YOU A...

KIDS ARE HERE

KIDS ARE FROM JUPITER

Kids Are from Jupiter

A GUIDE FOR PUZZLED PARENTS

MARK CHAMBERLAIN, PH.D.

SHADOW MOUNTAIN
SALT LAKE CITY, UTAH

Library of Congress Cataloging-in-Publication Data

Chamberlain, Mark D., 1964–
    Kids are from Jupiter / Mark D. Chamberlain
      p. cm.
    ISBN 1–57345–575–x (pbk.)
      1. Parent and child. 2. Child rearing. 3. Child development. I. Title.

HQ755.85.C47 1999
649'.1—dc21   99–053916

Printed in the United States of America   54459-6517

10 9 8 7 6 5 4 3 2

Contents

Part 3: Tricks of the Trade for Jovian Trainers

Part 4: Surviving an Invasion

Acknowledgments

When I'm struggling as a parent or as an advisor to parents, ideas and experiences that provide reassurance and insight stand out like precious gems among plain pebbles. Over the years, I've hoarded the brightest and most colorful, hoping for a format like this in which to share them. My sincere thanks to Emily Watts for her editorial guidance and to everyone else at Shadow Mountain who has helped sort, polish, and present this collection.

As I present these "gems," I make no pretense that they are my own. Many were uncovered on excursions with courageous clients. Still more were pointed out by my patient wife, Jenny, as we walked hand in hand along this sometimes bumpy road. She can see better than I through the dust that often covers the very best ones. Some came directly from my parents and "Mom and Dad Brown." (Of course, to them Jenny and I also owe our ability to recognize the rest.) Quite a number were displayed in the dazzling collections of fellow professionals. A few were lobbed in my direction by my sons, Ryan, Aaron, Alex, and Zachary.

Finally, quite an assortment was plucked from the generous palms of friends, relatives, schoolteachers, acquaintances, and complete strangers on street corners and at checkout stands. My sincere thanks to each one of you for your contribution to this book.

LITTLE STRANGERS FROM A STRANGE PLACE

One Sunday afternoon, I sat on our couch reading the newspaper as my son Ryan, then five years old, played with his stuffed Barney and Baby Bop toys at my feet. But the little dolls were not singing, "I love you, you love me, we're a happy family . . ." No. Barney, that rascal, had Baby Bop's little head clenched within his jaws. His tyrannosaurus instincts had apparently returned with a vengeance. The kind, gentle, chortling thing had all been an act. And it had worked. That unsuspecting little ceratopsian had been lulled into complacency by the crafty guy and was now paying the price. She had become Barney's dinner. He gnawed for a while until Baby Bop's little body went limp and lifeless.

Should I have been alarmed by this behavior? If this had been the only incident, I probably would have just brushed it off. But there's a pattern of this sort of thing with Ryan. For instance, I can't count the number of times I've played dead. I've been a mean buckin' bronco slain by a hunter. Been a woolly mammoth shot by sidewinder missiles and torpedoes. Been poisoned by cobras and rattlesnakes (who somehow manage to kill me with their rattles). Been a tiger in the jungle massacred by a machete.

None of this is my idea of fun. I'm cast in these roles by sons with wild and violent imaginations. And it's never a fair fight. Seems they always win, and I always, well . . . die.

I haven't always simply gone along with all this. At one time, heeding the warnings of some expert or advocacy group, I refused to buy them toy guns. But then they started shooting each other with bananas. One day they converted our toilet plunger into a machine gun. So I gave up the fight against my kids having toy guns, and before long I was recruited into fighting my kids using their toy guns.

But now Baby Bop was dead, and I felt like her blood was on my hands. *Should I be doing more?* I wondered. *Have I allowed my son to start down the wrong path of life? What shall I do about it now?*

I must admit, my concern stemmed in part from the fact that I'd seen this kind of pattern before—in the prisoners I counseled as a psychologist-in-training. The psychopaths of the bunch were often violent, had no remorse about their crimes, and viewed other people as objects for their use. I hate to say it, but at times this same personality profile fits my five-year-old pretty well. He hits his little brother. He doesn't seem to feel bad when he misbehaves or lies. And when it comes to family activities, his only interest is, "What's in it for me?"

With these concerns on my mind, I went back to reading the newspaper as Barney rose up from his kill to chase after a saber-toothed tiger (which looked suspiciously like Aaron's teddy bear). I checked out the *New York Times* bestseller list, as I usually do, and was reminded by John Gray, Ph.D., for the hundred and ninety-fourth week in a row, that men are from Mars and women are from Venus. That was when it hit me. If husbands and wives have a hard time getting along because they're from different planets, perhaps something like this also accounts for why it can be so hard to understand our kids. They must be from a planet even farther out in the solar system, nowhere close to where Mom and Dad come from. A planet with even stranger conditions and customs.

Kids are from Jupiter!

It's true, kids are from Jupiter. And since I've realized that they are, I no longer feel so confused. When something happens that would usually shake me, I remind myself, "That must be the way they're supposed to act *at their end of the galaxy.* That's probably quite common *on the fifth planet.*" I can't tell you what a relief this discovery has been.

There is one new problem now. Occasionally I have nightmares in which I'm abducted by aliens, transported from earth, and taken to live among millions of little Jovians (the guy at the planetarium tells me that's what they call natives of Jupiter). All in all, though, those bad dreams are a small price to pay for the peace of mind I now feel when I'm awake.

Now, I don't want to minimize the seriousness of violent behavior in children. If Ryan and his little brothers were in the habit of torturing grasshoppers or tying garbage to the tails of cats, I would definitely intervene. But I don't worry much about my kids' violent play anymore. They still seem fairly well-adjusted. For the most part, they limit their violence to the realm of fantasy, releasing vast quantities of pent-up energy in battles with imaginary enemies. They're kind and gentle the majority of the time.

The other day Ryan threatened me with a flashlight. "This weapon is very sharp and it's very laser and it will kill you to death."

"Oh, really?!" I feigned terror and hid behind a pillow. But in reality, I wasn't even fazed. I knew it must be a Jupiter thing.

YOU ARE HERE

KIDS ARE HERE

PART 1

How to Host an Alien

THERE ARE SCI-FI MOVIES *in which everyone on earth is annihilated in one blast. But those aren't the scariest ones. Most frightful are the ones in which parasite aliens leech onto or climb inside a human "host." Slowly they suck away life until the earthling is literally a shell of what it once was—a shell that the alien can then wear around as a protection against the earth's atmosphere and a disguise against its inhabitants. If this death-leech scenario doesn't fit your real-life experience as a parent, consider yourself fortunate. There are those of us who sometimes find life with kids to be just that unsettling.*

Even though we as parents might sometimes feel like "hosts" for parasitic little Jovians, there is a healthier way of going about the business of parenting. We can help our kids survive on this planet without losing our lifeblood or our sanity. We can start by remembering that they are unusual and delicate little creatures. Jovians have their quirks, Jupiter its unique set of habits and customs, so adjusting to Earth's atmosphere can be downright traumatic. Many kids experience "planet shock"—something on the order of culture shock but magnified tenfold.

Therefore, Jovians need our help, our patience, our empathy, and our tutoring. To be most effective as hosts, we must do more than provide a brief orientation to planet Earth: We must do everything we can to understand where the little aliens are coming from. As we observe our children and learn about them, the discoveries we make will be no less surprising than those made by sociologists exploring the customs of a remote culture or entomologists studying the habits of a bizarre species of insect. Just like these scientists, we must cultivate our curiosity and apply our powers of observation patiently and rigorously.

Of course, before our understanding of our children can deepen, we must first acknowledge that we don't yet fully know these creatures. We were kids ourselves not all that long ago, so we may start out assuming we know exactly what it's like for them because we have "been there, done that." However, once we arrived on Earth, our memory of our own planet-shock experiences began fading fast. Fortunately, that perspective can be restored as we spend time with our children and make a conscious effort to observe them. More empathy and compassion for our kids will follow, and we will be in a better position to handle the frustrations and challenges involved in raising them.

Some of the principles we explore in this book will hold true for most kids, but each child is unique. That is what makes Jupitology fascinating—full of surprises and rewards. So treat this book more as a field guide than a textbook or how-to manual. It may help you relax and enjoy the strange and sometimes wild experience of raising children. But it will be most helpful to the extent that it inspires you to study your own children and learn what makes them, in particular, tick. With it in hand and your child in sight, you have everything you need to conduct your own field study. To truly know these fascinating creatures is to love them, so I guarantee that once you begin your study of Jupitology, you'll be hooked for life.

Remember the Challenges of Childhood

"Y ou don't know how good you've got it," I overheard a father say to his young daughter as they walked through the shopping mall. It brought back memories of my childhood.

"Enjoy life now," Dad would say. "Someday you'll be an adult, and your life won't be so carefree."

There I would stand—a toddler, squeeze toy in hand, staring wide-eyed at Dad, trying to comprehend those sobering words.

Fortunately, Mom would intercede: "Take a break from balancing the checkbook if you need to, dear, but don't take your frustration out on the kids."

How soon we adults forget. Oh sure, you can remember the smell of your first dog, the taste of the sand in your sandbox, and even the name of your kindergarten teacher. Yet when it comes to the quality of your life as a child, your memory sputters and stalls. Instead of coming up blank, though, in place of your real childhood you're likely to find fabricated images that more closely resemble a fairy tale.

There's objective evidence that your childhood was not as carefree or easy as you remember it being. Just walk into your nearest grocery store and you'll find Exhibit A: those seats that are built into the grocery carts. They're quite simple, really: metal bars with a flat slab of plastic reminding you which store you're in. Not exactly La-Z-Boy comfort. The child is held in by one of the thin metal bars placed strategically between the legs. Do you remember ever trying to escape one of those carts? Of course not! This is evidence that the thin-metal-bar-between-the-legs design is a sound one—or evidence that you've forgotten the most painful parts of your childhood.

Since you no longer fit into those seats and you can't trust your memory, you'll never know for sure what your kids are going through when they sit in that grocery cart. The closest you can get now would be sitting on a barbecue grill or a gutter drainage grate. Try it out sometime (preferably when your neighbors aren't watching . . . and when there are no warm coals in the barbecue or water in the gutter). See if it brings back any memories. Then try to imagine sitting there for an hour or so while your mom or dad does the shopping.

Don't forget (well, I guess you already have!) that discomfort is not the only drawback to those seats. They also face backwards! The poor kids are uncomfortable *and* they can't see where they're going. No wonder so many kids scream in the grocery store. And no wonder they all look forward to kindergarten—it means no more grocery shopping.

Speaking of kindergarten, we can call that Exhibit B. That one school year alone provides overwhelming evidence that childhood is not all freedom. Little do kids know that riding backwards on a steel mesh seat is nothing compared to what awaits them in kindergarten. In kindergarten, children lose every freedom that legally can be denied by an adult whose patience has been worn thin by thirty-five years of bad "knock-knock" jokes. Retirement will be her salvation, and there are only 175 more kids standing in her way.

I'm kidding, of course, but the reality is that the key to survival in a classroom full of five-year-olds is rules. Rules are the next best thing to muzzles and leashes, which control kids much better but are much harder to justify on parent-teacher nights. In most kindergarten classes, there are two sets of rules. The first set is the formal list posted on the board and calmly discussed at the beginning of the year. The second set the teacher screams out when she goes into survival mode. Both sets have one thing in common: they are meant to restrict, and start with phrases like "Don't . . . ," "Never . . . ," and "So help me, if I catch you . . ."

What if, instead of all those restrictions, we gave kids even more freedom and power? For example, think how refreshing children would be to politics. Campaign posters would certainly be much cuter. And maybe the grown-up candidates would learn a lesson or two from their younger colleagues. Kids are less polished, but much nicer. They don't harbor grudges and save up ammunition for future mudslinging. If a kid is offended, he or she just bops the offender on the head with a Lincoln Log. Within five minutes the whole thing is forgotten. I'll bet you'd never hear one child candidate saying to another, "You're no Gerber baby. I knew the Gerber baby, and you're no Gerber baby."

It would be scary to liberate kids, though. Think of some of the other inevitable results: Nationwide revolts over school lunches. Brothers and sisters splitting up and fighting over who gets custody of the parents. Conscientious objectors walking out of junior high gym class.

It could get ugly. So let's keep true freedom away from kids after all. But let's also remember that being a kid is not the carefree, nonstop frolic we reminisce about. Next time you feel like pouting about the drudgeries of adult life, think twice before you whine to your kids about how great they have it. Take a moment and go sit on a gutter drainage grate. That should restore your empathy for children. And you'll be surprised how good your own life looks from down there.

Treat Life at Home As Your Kids' Aquarium

One of the most important things you can do as a parent is provide an adequate aquarium for your children. If you prefer more cuddly pets, don't worry. I'm not talking about an actual glass box full of water, rocks, and sea creatures. I'm speaking metaphorically here.

Now, with all due respect, in this metaphor our kids are the fish. (You and I both know we've called them worse in our weakest moments.) How our little fish fare in the great big ocean will be determined, in part, by what they are learning in the aquarium we create.

Every aquarium has its rules, make no mistake about it. And I'm not talking about the list that gets posted. I'm talking about the rules kids learn for surviving and getting what they want. For instance, in some aquariums, the little fish learn to be piranha. It's not that their parents are piranha or that they were born piranha. It's just that the grown-ups in the tank (that's you, Mom and Dad!) are strong enough and meaty enough that they don't seem to even miss the chunks of flesh that get torn from their bones.

Don't get me wrong, piranha aren't bad kids. At least, they don't intend to be. All fish, when they're small, take their share of chunks out of Mom and Dad. You see, if those kids could have things their way, Mom and Dad would give up their own lives and hand over control to the progeny.

But hopefully, before too long, we parents get tired of that kind of treatment and begin to protect ourselves. We recognize that we must be intact ourselves to be any good for our kids. And we see that life without limits is hard on them, too—ambiguous, uncertain, more than they can handle. So we take charge again. Someone has to do it, and during their reign we learned they're not ready for the job.

But what if we don't take charge of the aquarium? What if we know things are out of hand but have solemnly sworn not to be as harsh as our own parents were? What if we bought into some expert's assurance that kids contain only goodness and light? What if we've been spooked by all the talk about the thousands of ways we can damage their self-esteem? What if we're still holding out for the metamorphosis, waiting for our tolerance and long-suffering to deliver well-behaved—not to mention self-actual-ized—children?

Well, then we'll just keep raising piranha. Because as good as those child-centered philosophies sound, kids need firm guidance.

One immediate problem with raising piranha is that job satis-faction hits rock bottom. (In fact, Mom and Dad themselves might just hit rock bottom, ending up lifeless among those colorful little pebbles in the depths of the tank.)

However, the effect on us is not the worst problem. Tough as we are, we usually live through it. Our little fish are the ones who really suffer. Later, when they make their way out to the ocean, they're in for it, because the rules there are quite different. Needless to say, piranha are not very popular. And out in the ocean, unlike in the aquarium, no one feels obligated to put up with them. Friends don't tolerate someone who demands and demands while giving nothing in return. Bosses soon fire employ-ees who won't swim as they're told.

Parents need to remember, it's their aquarium, and they make the rules. Whatever we do at home, our little ones will expect the same treatment in the ocean. We need to tame the piranha in our children while we can—if not for our own survival, for theirs. Firm guidance won't kill them. In fact, it may be what helps them someday weather the waves and the coral and the salt water of the real world.

Treat Time with Your Kids As Their Apprenticeship for Life

How important is spending time together as a family? Think of it this way: Our kids are on apprenticeship. The "profession" they are learning is getting along in the world. How else will they develop the skills they need, if not by spending time with us? We are their expert consultants, already doing what they need to learn.

In my work with youth and their families, quite often I have the opportunity to do a psychological assessment, during which I sit down with a teenager for a one- to two-hour interview. We discuss a wide range of topics in these interviews, and often I explore their entire history. I talk with their parents and sometimes with their schoolteachers, and I look through pages and pages of other experts' opinions about these kids.

I have discovered in these assessments that I gain the most information about the youth and their chances for future success when we discuss one particular topic: the quantity and quality of the time they have spent with other family members, especially their parents. The evidence suggests overwhelmingly that spending time together with family members is an important key to a young person's happiness, ability to cope with challenges, and sense of self.

How can children learn to handle a wide variety of situations and solve many different kinds of problems? There's no better way than by watching their parents and siblings handle a wide variety of situations and solve many different kinds of problems. Of course, this opportunity is available only when family members spend hours and hours around each other.

Some of the kids I work with have been neglected. Their parents have failed to provide adequate care and supervision. Because they haven't spent much time with their parents, they are at a serious disadvantage in handling day-to-day life. When they confront unfamiliar circumstances, they feel anxious and unsure of themselves. With no reservoir of knowledge and confidence to draw from, they have difficulty coping with even the smallest of challenges.

On the other hand, as I talk with kids who have spent time with their parents—even doing seemingly insignificant things—I am impressed at their competence. Little things like "playing together at the park," "going to Cub Scouts with Dad," "helping Mom run errands," and "going on family trips to Colorado to visit our relatives" seem to provide the opportunity to learn important lessons of life.

Plus, there are those brief snatches of togetherness sprinkled throughout the day that we as parents hardly notice: a few moments in the front room watching for the school bus in the morning or a little chat at bedtime before the children drift off to sleep. These may seem like tiny building blocks now. But they do provide a basis for future growth. And as the years pass, these tiny building blocks may just form the deepest foundations for our children's highest pursuits.

Remember That Kids Learn through Repetition

If raising kids were a track-and-field event, it would be a marathon with hurdles, run on a circular track. We face challenge after challenge and then return to cycle through the same challenges again.

We teach our kids honesty, for example, and insist that they tell the truth. But when a four-year-old has a choice between displeasing Mom and Dad and telling a bold-faced lie—"I didn't eat that cookie"—you can count on being lied to. And don't feel like you've failed in your role as a parent. Believe me, there will be hundreds of opportunities for your child to improve his or her truth-telling record in the future. That's the great thing about teaching kids. It's almost never too late to circle back around and work on a particular problem or developmental issue again. In fact, that's the way kids learn—by repetition.

We can take comfort in this: If our kids don't get it right this time, don't worry, they'll have the chance again soon to do better! It's like watching *The Andy Griffith Show*—if you miss something important, just wait around. There will be a rerun of this episode.

We all hope our kids will develop into decent adults someday. Okay, let's be honest, we're hoping they'll be *exceptional*. It's okay to have high expectations for our kids. But it's also imperative that we allow room for them to grow. We can do so by communicating what we'd like them to become, but in a way that doesn't make them feel ashamed that they're not there yet.

Since our kids are bound to repeat their errors, we should

view each mistake they make as a step, not as a failed outcome. Once we are open to this perspective, we discover that blunders provide the perfect chance to strengthen our child's understanding of the rule he or she broke. The following strategy, suggested by Glenn Latham, can be particularly helpful in doing so.

Suppose Susie has broken a family rule by straying too far out of the neighborhood to play. Ask her what she *should* have done: "What do I expect of you?" If she answers correctly, praise her for that. If she focuses on a sibling's or friend's misdeeds, acknowledge this quickly and then return the focus to her behavior: "It may be that Carleen went outside the neighborhood, but what do I expect of you?"

"I should stay on our street."

"Excellent, I'm pleased that you remember!"

If Susie still doesn't get what she did wrong, do some gentle teaching (perhaps for the fifth time). "You can only play on *our* street." And then always give her the chance to give you feedback about her understanding: "What's the rule?"

"I can't go past the corner."

"Excellent!"

You may talk about what was so appealing on the next street. You may take away the privilege of playing outside for a day or two. But don't expect that one intervention will necessarily solve the problem for good.

This is one of the (too many) ways moms are naturally better at raising kids than dads. Most moms view single incidents as just that—one in a series of almost countless interactions. Dads tend to view each conflict as a potential Waterloo. "If we let this one go, that will be the end of it. This child will know he can walk all over us."

I joined the South Davis Junior High track team as a complete novice. I remember watching the 220-yard hurdles for the first time with a veteran (ninth-grade) teammate. Going around the first turn, two of the runners upended hurdles in their lanes. "How many points do they lose for that?" I asked.

"You don't lose points for knocking over a hurdle," my teammate responded.

"How many seconds are added on to your time, then?" I asked.

"Oh, no. It usually slows you down a little. And it may kill your knee! But you're not penalized for it, no matter how many hurdles you knock down during the race. The important thing is not to get distracted, because there's going to be another hurdle right away, and you have to be ready for that one."

Remember that the same thing is true in our work as parents: You don't lose points for goofing up. Instead of the last one, focus on the next hurdle, because it is coming right up.

Teach Them to Talk Out Their Feelings

Emotions are not always as neat and tidy as we'd like them to be. As parents, for example, we're well aware that it's not unusual to feel both love and anger toward the same person—we won't mention any names. One of the most valuable lessons we can teach our children is how to tolerate such ambivalent feelings. We do so primarily by encouraging them to talk out their emotions.

I once worked with a twelve-year-old, Kristen, who had spent years in foster care. Steve and Kelly, her group home "parents" for the past two years, were moving out of the group home to a house of their own. They were arranging to take Kristen with them as a foster child. Kristen was excited because she would be getting more attention. Steve and Kelly had three kids of their own, but now they wouldn't be taking care of seven other teenage girls as they had in the group home. Kristen felt special because she was the one going with them. She also expressed her excitement about this arrangement being "more like a regular family."

Although Kristen eagerly anticipated the change initially, about three weeks before the move she started to get anxious. Her behavior deteriorated, and she was more defiant at home and at school. Wednesday afternoon when we met for our weekly therapy session, I could see she wasn't her usual self. She sat rigid, arms folded, a pillow propped in her lap like a shield between us.

As she began talking, she expressed apprehension about the change. "This isn't going to work out. I can't move with Steve and Kelly."

"How come?" I inquired.

"They want me to share their soap and shampoo with them."

"It's a foster home," I replied. "Instead of sharing your personal things with all the other girls, as you have been, you'll share them with the Johnsons. Just like in a real family."

"I already *have* a real family!" Kristen demanded. "You only share shampoo and soap with your family, and Steve and Kelly are *not* my family!"

I finally clued in to Kristen's ambivalence. She eagerly anticipated her move to a new home and was excited to be treated more like a daughter by the Johnsons. However, her feelings were mixed. As she moved closer to their family, she felt like she was abandoning her own.

Her anxiety wasn't really about soap and shampoo. So we stopped talking about the details of the living arrangements and talked instead about the turmoil she was going through emotionally. At first, this was difficult for Kristen to do. To her it seemed she could have only one emotion about the move. Previously she had felt only excitement. But when she felt she was abandoning her family, anxiety dominated, and she concluded, "This isn't going to work out."

With encouragement, Kristen explored the possibility that all of her feelings were valid. She could be excited *and* anxious about the move. She could enjoy getting closer to the Johnsons and still love her own family and regret that she was not with them. By the time we were done, I noticed a drastic change in Kristen's body language—her posture had relaxed and there was a smile on her face.

If they can't talk it out, kids are likely to act out their emotional turmoil. A good reminder phrase when young kids are throwing a tantrum is "Use your words." This can help them learn to weather a storm of emotions and regain control. By expressing their feelings as they talk with us, our kids are often becoming aware of such emotions for the very first time themselves. When we see the telltale signs of emotional storminess, we can even help our kids out by giving them words for what they're feeling: "You're angry at Mom right now." "You're worried about going to a new class." "You're sad that your friends left you out."

Talking things out this way does not make difficult feelings go away. It does help calm the turmoil, though. We can help our children find peace of mind if we can acknowledge their feelings, tolerate difficult emotions ourselves, and assure our kids it's okay to talk them out.

Respect Their Internal Set of Rules

Kids have two sets of rules to juggle, two sets of demands they must balance somehow. One set is handed down from external authority figures like parents and teachers. The other set is "handed up," if you will, from forces that act as internal authorities of sorts—their own needs and drives and fears.

We make things a lot easier on our kids and ourselves if we don't pit our rules against their needs. We can do so by observing our children carefully, identifying their internal rules, and taking care to avoid, whenever possible, making conflicting demands.

When we do fight with our child's internal authorities, we almost always lose. I was reminded of this one night when I was putting the kids to bed. The two older boys were being noisy in their room, which is right next to the baby's room. I sent Aaron, the two-year-old, into Mom and Dad's bed, saying, "When you can both settle down, Aaron can come back into his own bed."

Ryan protested, "I'll be lonely, Dad!"

"Both of you keep quiet, and he'll be right back in," I reassured him. "Don't get off your bed, or it will take even longer." As I left the room, Ryan continued to plead, and I realized that my order might be too difficult for him to follow.

By the time I returned to the family room, I looked back to see that Ryan was standing at the door of his room. I knew that the internal authority of his loneliness had overpowered my external authority. Ryan doesn't like risking more punishment. However, that was the lesser of two evils in this case. It was even worse to remain alone in the room when he's used to falling asleep in his brother's company. Recognizing that, I decided to let it go and just wait to see what would happen.

For the next fifteen minutes the boys were as quiet as mice. When I returned to their room, Aaron was back in his bed. Ryan was holding up a book and quietly describing the pictures. "I went into your room, Dad," Ryan confessed. "I told Aaron if he'd come back in I'd read books with him."

"Read books," Aaron said, smiling.

Ryan had worked it out so that he could satisfy my demand for quiet at the same time he satisfied his own desire for company. I was relieved at that point that I hadn't followed through on my initial plan, which would have achieved only one of those goals. On second thought, it probably would not have even done that—after all, a lonely four-year-old may not have been the most quiet four-year-old.

Whenever we can, we must avoid fighting against the needs that drive a hard bargain from inside a child. When we battle them, we're swimming upstream. Someone is bound to lose: usually it's the parent, but if the parent does prevail, the child loses out on having an important need met. Also, since developmental needs are, by nature, powerful forces, we generally spend more energy on the issue than it's really worth to us.

In the work I do with parents of older kids, I often see them doing the same thing I did that night: making demands of their kids that conflict with those children's internal needs. Some of the primary directives a teenager receives from his or her internal authority are "be your own person; prove you don't need others; stand on your own." Therefore, when we say, "As long as you're in my house, you'll do things my way!" we may set up a no-win situation for our kids. They're left to decide whether they will disappoint us and risk punishment or end up feeling like they wimped out and caved in by submitting to us.

Fourteen-year-old Robert was brought in for treatment because he was acting "very strange." He reminded his mother of the way his uncle acted right before he was institutionalized for the treatment of a severe mental illness. Lately Robert had been irritable and more withdrawn than ever from the family; he seemed always to have a chip on his shoulder. He spent most of his time at home alone in his room listening to music or talking on the phone with friends from school. At times his mom and dad insisted that he join the rest of the family, but then it seemed he tried to make their time together miserable.

So far this sounds like a typical teenager, right? These are all changes that parents of adolescents ought to expect. Teens are developing their own sense of identity. They are just beginning to test their wings, evaluating how they fit into the world as separate and unique individuals.

However, Robert had more serious problems. Perhaps most troubling to his mom, recently Robert had begun picking fights at school and at home, particularly with his eleven-year-old brother, Val. Val usually stood up to him, and their conflicts were ending in fistfights. Dad broke them up when he was home, but Mom was afraid to get into the middle of them—she was quite petite, and both boys were now bigger and stronger than she. It was time to get some outside help.

Mom reported that she had been trying to reassert her position of authority with Robert, but with little success. She described trying in every way she could to "bring him under control." "You need to listen to me!" she'd say, or "I'm your mother; do as I say!"

I had nothing against the way she was handling the situation, in theory. If it works, I don't see anything wrong with communicating your anger and raising your voice to let kids know you're serious. But it wasn't working (and often it doesn't), so it seemed to me that we ought to try a new approach.

In a broad sense, Mom was frustrated because Robert seemed to be diverging from the path she wanted him to follow. Her method for getting him "back on track" was to demand that he comply with her requests. In a way, this set up a dilemma for Robert. For the most part, kids—even teenagers—want to please their parents. But if Robert complied with his mother's demands, he might be disobeying the rules of his internal authority: "Be your own person; prove you don't need others; stand on your own." Giving in to his mother's demands might feel like wimping out to Robert.

When we understand our teenagers' developmental needs, we as parents can use this knowledge to our advantage—and ultimately to theirs. We can deemphasize rather than underscore the power difference between us. Rather than "I'm your mother, do as I say!" we can adopt the attitude of "Let's look at *our* problem here and see what *we* can figure out."

Furthermore, instead of concentrating on what seem to be the differences between our own goals and theirs, we can systematically search for the ever-present areas of overlap. For example, if we know our teenagers want to take more charge of their lives, we can avoid framing our requests in ways that imply that their compliance means handing control of their lives back over to us.

Here's how Robert's mother and I made this shift in the way we approached his problems. We decided to try to make anger *inconsistent* with being in control of his own life, rather than *the way* he asserted control. After discovering that Robert loved to play "commando tactics" with his buddies at the park and war games on his computer, I likened the anger that welled up inside him and prompted his outbursts to a sniper. "Every time you act out your anger, the sniper has just pegged you," I suggested.

As Robert considered this new way of looking at his anger problem, I explained: "Anger is a very powerful enemy, and many people my age and older have not yet learned to avoid falling prey to it. However, even the cleverest of enemies, even the most skilled Navy Seals or Green Berets, sometimes send out warning signals. What kinds of warnings might they send?"

Robert suggested that they might snap a twig or be wearing camouflage that doesn't quite fit their surroundings.

"Now, what about the sniper Anger?" I asked. "What kinds of warning signs might he send out when he is intending to nail you?"

Robert thought for a long time. "Well," he said, "sometimes I can feel my face start to burn right before I blow up."

"Before *he* blows you up, you mean," I said, attempting again to frame his anger as something external, something he could gain some distance from and control over.

"Yeah. And sometimes my brother starts picking a fight, and I know Anger is right around the corner then."

"Excellent!" I cheered. I got out some paper for us to take some notes on. Before the session was over, we had made a list of six warning signs that gave away the sniper Anger's impending attack.

"Sometimes there will be no warning," I acknowledged as we ended our meeting. "But as you pay attention to when you get pegged and keep track of what happens leading up to those attacks, I think you will get better at avoiding falling prey to this enemy of yours. I really think you are a better soldier than he is. Let's see how it goes this week."

We dubbed Mom an "ally" in Robert's battle against anger. His father, who had in the past had some difficulty managing his own anger, became a "veteran" who could be consulted for strategic advice. Of course, Robert may be struggling to control his anger to this day, but that change in perspective provided some immediate relief to him and his family. The intensity of their conflicts decreased that very week.

When we try to assert our control as parents in a blatant show of force, one of two things can happen. Our kids may give in, but then their own need for autonomy is not met. They submit, but in the process they become weaker instead of stronger as people. Later, when they hook up with a peer or a boyfriend or girlfriend who has a domineering personality, they may be in real trouble.

The other thing that may happen is that our kids accept our challenge, and the tug-of-war is on. The tough get going, and they carry their displays of independence even further than they had before, further than they had initially intended.

Helping our children assert more control in their own lives, especially over the temptation to defy us, is much better than either of these options. And we can do this best when we respect and help them meet their developmental needs.

Don't Be Alarmed by Their Defiance

Thirteen-year-old Kevin was giving his parents fits. He was a bright boy who was an underachiever in school. The combination of long hair and shaved spots on his head was most unattractive—at least, his mom and dad thought so. His music was too loud, his pants were too baggy, and he wore too much jewelry and in all the wrong places.

These declarations of independence were quite disconcerting to Kevin's parents. They were very worried. They had some idea about the lifestyles of the adults whose appearance he was imitating. He painted anarchy symbols on his shoes, for instance, and they'd never met a grown anarchist who was a productive member of society.

There are plenty of reasons to worry about kids, especially teenagers like Kevin. But if we take a step back and look at the big picture, there's also plenty to ease our minds.

For starters, consider this: When was the last time you heard a president of the United States, in one of his speeches, insist that we really are independent from England? Doesn't happen. Hasn't for more than a century. Why? Because now we're confident about our power as a nation. Our autonomy is no longer in question. So we, as a nation, are more relaxed about it than we were two hundred years ago.

Kids like Kevin, on the other hand, remind me a lot of Patrick Henry, hero of the American Revolution: "Give me liberty or give me death!" That's how important freedom is to them. In fact, there are a lot of parallels between typical teenagers and the founding fathers of our country. In their own way, teenagers carry around their flags declaring, "Don't tread on me!" If too much is demanded of them, they may just dump some tea into the harbor.

Most adults, on the other hand, are more like the leaders of our country today. They don't go around insisting that they don't *have* to do what their boss asks of them. They and everyone else are well aware of that fact. But they've decided to do what their boss demands anyway. They don't much like the alternative.

Most ten- and eleven-year-olds don't understand that there are alternatives. When someone in authority asks them to do something, they typically comply. They are very concrete in their understanding of relationships and options.

Sometime around age twelve or thirteen, however, a whole new world opens up. A parent or teacher makes a request, and suddenly "no" has become a possibility to consider. Realizing this, many teenagers, at least for a time, use "no" indiscriminately— simply because now they can. They seem to like the very sound of it. They practice it all the time and become quite adept at its use and abuse.

Eventually, however, if things go right, it gets old. If no one overreacts, they realize that people respect their power to choose—within certain limits, at least. Then, "no" is no longer for every occasion, and neither are their combat boots and baggy pants. They've practiced "no" enough that they're comfortable with it as an option. When you ask more mature teenagers to do something, they don't immediately scream, "NO!" at the top of their lungs. Instead they think, "maybe, maybe not." This is mature thinking, the hallmark of adulthood: deciding for oneself and taking responsibility for those choices. Self-government. Not anarchy.

Protect Them from Too Much TV

The other day I was talking to my friend Gitti, who's from Austria, about kids and TV. "Experts in our country say that too much TV is not good for children, so I let Philip and Martina watch only a half hour a day," she said.

Martina is six, Philip five. I'd met them before and talked with them, though they didn't seem to understand much of my English. I'd also seen them playing around the apartment complex. Philip is usually chattering away at Dad, helping with the chores, or chasing a cat into a stairwell. Martina spends her time hanging close to Mom, splashing in the pool, or reading picture books. They don't seem like kids who would be much interested in TV. But only a half hour a day?

"That's funny," I responded. "Experts in our country also say that too much TV is not good for children. We Americans let our children watch about three hours a day."

The research finding that too much TV is not good for kids is there—has been for years. But it seems that when it comes to TV and kids, our practices aren't keeping pace with our understanding. For those of us who could use a refresher course on the effect of the tube on our youngsters, here's a quick summary.

First, the good news: A picture can be worth a thousand words in sparking the interest of kids, both young and old. Kids can learn to be more polite by watching Barney and Mr. Rogers. The Teletubbies can show them that the world is an interesting place. They can improve their language skills and learn to do some basic math by watching *Sesame Street*.

But there is also bad news. One potent pitfall of the medium relates to its greatest strength: TV provides an avenue for kids to learn indirectly about nature and parts of the world that they would not be able to experience firsthand. And thus the hazard: Heavy viewers tend to settle into such second-hand experiencing as a way of life. Violence and sexual content are no less dangerous for being experienced indirectly. Kids take what they see on TV very seriously. Even if they understand intellectually that "it's not real," their bodies respond to the excitement of television as if it were. As our kids watch, their minds are being influenced, their tastes are being programmed, and their attention spans are being shortened. Some in the entertainment industry may deny it, but there are reams of research reports documenting that watching violence on TV really does promote aggression in children. Research further documents that the kids who watch the most TV are also the most likely to view the world as a "mean and scary place."

One of the most disturbing influences of TV on kids has been chronicled by media critic Michael Medved. Medved has pointed out that those who produce TV, movies, and other forms of media today are engaged in nothing short of an assault on the American family. Many of their messages are antithetical to family values. And he's not referring only to sex or violence here, but to how the media attacks the family in more subtle ways as well. Consider, for example, how TV and movies portray parents and other adults: They're often shown as bumbling idiots who rely on the much brighter children to save the day. Certainly such depictions undermine our efforts as parents to guide our children.

Expert opinions and scientific research aside, the simple fact is this: The more time our kids spend in front of the TV, the more someone besides us is determining the ideas and images to which they're exposed. Television programming is as persuasive in teaching values as television commercials are in luring consumers. David Frost has pointed out that "television is an invention that permits you to be entertained in your own living room by people you wouldn't have in your home." If we wouldn't even have some of these folks in our home, should we be allowing them to help us raise our children?

The other day I saw a cartoon that offered an intriguing idea: When TV becomes an information superhighway, maybe we can send some of the garbage back. For now, though, it's a one-way, dead-end street that will channel all its traffic into our homes, if we let it. We each have access to a remote-control "Do Not Enter" sign. Fortunately for Martina and Philip, their mom uses it.

Don't Be Afraid to Deprive Them Some

We live in an age of indulgence. Unlike most other members of our species who have walked on this earth, we are strangers to deprivation. Instead of emptiness—empty stomachs or empty heads—we are full to the top and overflowing. We have too much of almost everything, and we keep trying to cram even more into our lives. We turn up the volume. We keep accruing recreational equipment. We work longer hours to make more money. We put a television in the kitchen so we never have to be without. We see more doctors for our ever-increasing aches and pains. We have cellular phones so we can talk without sitting still. We have more information than we can ever sort through, and it's more accessible—right at our fingertips. More radio stations to choose from. More places to be and more ways to get there.

Now we have everything, but somehow it's not quite enough. We have found that more is less. We are awash with "sexual freedom," yet parched from the lack of love in our lives. We can communicate with almost anyone on the planet, but to do so we must sit alone in front of a machine. We have more cars per family so that each of us can go his or her own separate way. Our menu options have multiplied, but none of it tastes quite as good as it used to. We see more psychotherapists, yet we're more disturbed than ever.

Because we now have more than ever, we're surprised that our kids aren't satisfied. We keep pouring into an overflowing bucket, and then we wonder why they don't find their lives more fulfilling, why they don't have more self-esteem.

The truth is, less is sometimes more. In the words of a traditional Korean proverb, "Hunger is the best side dish." We more fully appreciate what we have after being deprived of it for a time. Goodies have to be missing to be missed, and they have to be missed to be fully appreciated.

Kim Anderson is one of the psychology professors at Ricks College, where I used to teach. Every semester Kim taught her students to train baby chicks to perform skills you'd never expect from these "lower life forms." One Monday morning, I watched her trying to train one of the chicks. Every time it turned to the left, she slid in a little tray of grain for it to eat. Her goal was to eventually get it to turn in a complete circle. During the time I watched, the chick didn't learn much. Occasionally, by chance, it would turn to the left, but it didn't deliberately repeat that action to get the food. Exasperated, Kim finally decided to end the training session. "Feel right here," she said to me, placing my hand on the baby chick's gullet. It was bulging with grain. "This chick has already had too much to eat. It won't perform for me because it's not hungry." She went on to explain that the weekend lab assistant had misunderstood her directions and fed all the chicks their normal diet that weekend. They had not been deprived, so offering food as an incentive did not motivate them to learn.

Fat and satisfied lab rats won't learn a maze to get food. Wild animals hand-fed by tourists soon lose their hunting skills. And what's true across the rest of the animal kingdom is just as true for teenagers and toddlers.

Teresa was a fourteen-year-old "delinquent" who had, among other things, chosen not to attend school. In fact, she had not shown up to a single class for over a year when she first arrived at the group home where I consulted. Teresa's mother, exhausted by her own failures, said "Good luck" to the new foster parents as she turned her daughter over. She added, "I've tried everything. Nothing will motivate her."

Having watched other kids come into the group home, I must admit I was not quite as surprised as her mother two weeks later when Teresa attended an entire day of school in exchange for a single can of Pepsi. What had changed? For two weeks she had been deprived of all the luxuries of adolescence: Nintendo, free time with friends, television, dessert, and money she had not worked for. Those well-earned cans of Pepsi were the best drink she had ever tasted.

Teresa's mother had tried to offer her everything, and was confused when she responded with defiance. Teresa did not appreciate what she had; she hadn't had to work for it. Deprivation changed her attitude and her behavior in just a short time. Less had become more for Teresa.

We've been taught that doing our job right as parents will result in happy children. As I heard Elizabeth Ellis, a clinical psychologist from Atlanta, once say, "Parents don't seem to see themselves as the teachers of skills but rather as the creators of happiness." In this age where the customer is always right, we want our kids to be satisfied with the product we offer them.

"You know, I'm really concerned about little Karen. She doesn't like school."

She's probably fine—just learning to do something difficult. How well that will serve her later in life when she doesn't really like her job, but can make the most of it until she finds something better. Or when she's dissatisfied in her marriage, and can get to work finding solutions instead of giving up.

"It's a real problem. Tommy gets angry whenever I ask him to do chores around the house."

That doesn't sound so unusual. But it can be very troubling to parents who want their kids to be satisfied. And it can scare them right out of demanding that their children measure up.

"Okay, okay. Whatever will make you happy. Go ahead and do what you want. I don't want to be the bad guy anymore."

Wrong. Being the bad guy is part of being a parent. As I look around the buffet table we provide our children, it seems they have more than enough of all but one side dish. They don't get enough deprivation. Perhaps this is why they just can't seem to get enough of everything else even when they've had too much. Perhaps this is how kids with so much going on could describe themselves as "bored." More is more only up to a point, and when we try to give our kids everything we catapult them right past that mark, which leaves them where they are now, with so much more and so much less.

CELEBRATE COMPETENCE

$\int$ ome time ago I worked with seventeen-year-old Elaine, who had some serious problems. At the time, she lived in a group home with five other girls. Her parents had given custody of her over to the state because they couldn't handle her at home.

Elaine fought continually with her two sisters, complained about her mom (nothing she did was ever enough), hated and would not talk to her stepdad, was failing her junior year of high school, and at least once a week talked about how hopeless she felt and how she intended to commit suicide. When she lived at home there was one incident in which she drove the family truck up into the mountains and totaled it by driving it off a ten-foot embankment.

When I started working with Elaine, she spent the first two months of our weekly sessions trying to convince me she needed to go back to the psychiatric ward of the local hospital, where she had been for the previous month. It became clear to me that she liked the hospital because of all the attention and concern the staff there had given her. She said the therapists and the nurses there were always willing to talk when she was feeling down, and on days when she was really depressed or suicidal, they would spend one-on-one time with her, taking walks and trying to help her cope with her emotions and feel better.

After a month in the hospital she was feeling just as depressed as she had been on admittance and was more suicidal than ever. However, due to the high cost, her caseworker insisted she couldn't stay in the hospital forever. At some risk, her family decided to move her out to a less restrictive and less expensive treatment setting. That was how she came to the group home where I consulted.

Although she felt her situation was desperate and she needed to return to the hospital, eventually she realized I wasn't going to recommend she be sent back. I'll bet I repeated a hundred times, "I know it feels like you can't make it here, but your parents and your caseworker and the doctors in the hospital really believe in you and feel like you can do it." I don't know that this was true. I do know that the expense of staying at the hospital was prohibitive.

Every week, sometimes twice a week, I'd get a call from the group home parents. For example, Ron, the group home dad, called one day and said: "Elaine feels like killing herself. She was tempted to jump out in front of the oncoming traffic today on her way home from the bus stop after school. I'm staying with the other girls; Brenda's with her. She took her for a ride up the canyon in the van. Hopefully she'll be able to relax there and get a little perspective."

At other times the group home parents called and said: "Elaine's feeling very depressed and says she can't wait for Thursday for her therapy session. Can you talk with her on the phone?" I'd do twenty minutes of therapy over the phone with her.

In addition to treating her depression, as a treatment team we tried to understand Elaine's experience and help her develop better ways of getting what she wanted. We identified as a primary problem Elaine's lack of initiative. As we tried to piece together her history, it seemed to us that she had not experienced the safety and freedom to be a kid when she was younger. Her mom was a single parent who was only sixteen when she had Elaine, and Elaine hadn't received much nurturing from her mom. In fact, when Elaine had two little sisters, her mom would sometimes go out for long periods of time and leave four-year-old Elaine there to take care of things. So whereas most kids spend much of their childhood as passive recipients of love and nurturing and other goodies, Elaine had found herself saddled with grown-up responsibilities long before she was ready for them.

In fact, the psychiatric ward of the hospital had been one of the first chances for her to adopt a more passive stance while the staff and doctors "treated" her, fed her, and took care of her needs. Adopting the patient role was tremendously soothing to Elaine, and given her background it's easy to see why. However, during her time there, she also discovered that the hospital staff abided by several unwritten rules: (1) The better you do, the sooner you'll leave—which was no incentive for Elaine because she liked it there; (2) if you say things are fine, your therapy time will be cut short; and (3) you get more of the staff's time and attention when you're depressed.

Well, if Elaine had to be "sick" or "dysfunctional" to get the attention, she was certainly able to do that. In fact, the group home parents started noticing that if someone else had nightmares and was given attention, Elaine began having nightmares with content that was even more horrendous. She often had stomachaches and headaches that kept her home from school. Even when she went to school, she complained to her teachers about physical and psychological ailments of all varieties.

Obviously, this pattern had been gathering steam for some time. Her hospital stay had certainly not been the cause of Elaine's "take care of me!" attitude; it was simply an environment where this mode of operation had paid off.

As we tried to determine the best way to treat Elaine, we felt like we were in a bind. We couldn't just cut off the payoff she received from others when her problems got more serious—when someone says she's suicidal, you don't say "talk to me when you're cheerful"! We considered sharing with her our interpretation of the problem, pointing out to her that she seemed to extort attention from people by talking about problems that were impossible to ignore.

In the end, we decided on the following course of action: Whenever she demonstrated competence, we'd dwell on it and not let it drop. When we were talking with her about suicide and depression and nightmares, we'd avoid eye contact and seem preoccupied and yawn now and then. But when she talked about anything that resembled successful coping, we'd become more interested and animated.

We recognized that if we wanted this to work, we would have to continue to shower her with attention—it seemed to us that she was emotionally wounded and she needed more nurturing than the typical teenager. But we decided to make the most intense attention contingent upon competence instead of sickness.

With Elaine, at first it seemed that there was no competence on which to dwell. I remember one of the staff members at the group home, Rhonda, helping her get a volunteer job for the final month of summer vacation. It was like pulling teeth: Rhonda brought home the application, held Elaine's hand through the process of filling it out, took it back and turned it in for her, and even coached her through the interview. Due more to Rhonda's effort than her own, Elaine did get the job.

Well, it was volunteer work, so the expectations of her boss and manager were low to begin with. But she struggled to meet even those. In fact, she let down her manager several times, coming in for work late and at times failing to show up at all.

For many other teenagers, this performance would probably have been considered a failure. And I remember that in staff meetings, that was the way we talked about it. We did notice, however, that during that period of volunteer work Elaine was using up less of the staff members' time talking about depression and suicide.

I recall in particular the therapy session I had with Elaine immediately following the completion of this job. School was about to start, and we were reviewing how the summer had gone for her. When she said things were somewhat better now and that she was feeling more energetic, I was about to say, "Well, then, I'll see you next week," and move on to my session with another girl in the home. But I caught myself. I realized, *This is the kind of competence we wanted Elaine to demonstrate, and now she's doing it.* Instead of dismissing Elaine, I said, "You're feeling good, you've completed a summer job: Let's go celebrate!" I drove her down to the Purple Turtle drive-in and we ordered some raspberry shakes and french fries.

We talked primarily about her job, and during that conversation I learned just how much it had meant to her. It had been a real effort for her to go to work, but having a job had made her feel important, so she had persevered. Interacting with the other employees was awkward, and she thought they would think she was crazy or weird because she had been in a psych ward in the hospital and now lived in a group home. She woke up many mornings with a stomachache from worrying about how it would go, but most mornings she fought through it and went anyway. Many times throughout that month she had been tempted to just give up, but each time she had decided to keep trying. It became clear to me just how difficult this had been for her, and that her apparently lackluster performance really was an improvement from where she had been. She was blazing new ground, and it wasn't easy. I had almost missed her success because it looked so much like someone else's failure.

Sensing the magnitude of this recent success and its poignancy for Elaine, I felt privileged and excited to be there celebrating with her. I asked her all kinds of questions about everything that had anything to do with her competence. We talked about how early she had to wake up to catch the bus, and what a struggle it was to do so. About the route the bus took, and how nervous she was at first about catching the right bus and getting off at the right stop. About the courage it took to keep the job when it would have been much easier to quit. About what her boss was like. About how her boss was satisfied with the work she did. About how nice it would be to have her boss as a reference when she was looking for work in the future. About her co-workers, and in particular about one co-worker with whom she had had an argument, and about how much bravery it had taken to go to work and be around her the next day. About the work she did planting flowers and weeding. About how she helped care for the plants in the center islands on one stretch of road with which I was familiar. About her work on a park where I used to take my kids. About one of my first jobs, caring for the grounds of an Italian restaurant. About yard work I'd done since then. About how she was now prepared to care for the yard if she ever had a house of her own. "You're fortunate," I said. "We just moved into our house a few months ago, and I have to put in a yard this year." She told me to get rid of all the weeds before I planted, so that they wouldn't grow back in with the grass.

I'm sure the folks in the booth next to us at the drive-in had no idea this was psychotherapy. And as I describe it, you may be questioning that yourself. But think about the experience for Elaine: Someone was asking her about the details of something she did well and about the personality attributes and strengths that enabled her to do it. How much better it was to talk about all this than to talk in the same kind of detail about her headaches and her nightmares and her personality flaws and her depression and her suicidal thoughts!

We continued this kind of emphasis in the work we did together. It became much more pleasant to work with her, and I was impressed with the progress she continued to make. Hopefully, in the future, Elaine will be a little less likely to be overwhelmed by problems. When stress hits, she has something she can do besides focusing on her symptoms and her negative reactions to them. She can dwell on her competence and coping skills. Last I heard, school was going better for Elaine and she was involved in an "explorer program" after school, in which teenagers shadow police officers to learn more about their work and get a better feel for what a job in law enforcement would be like.

Thinking about Elaine now makes me wonder why it took me and the rest of the staff months to change our focus from pathology and problems to coping and competence. It seems that all kids have certain competencies, strengths, skills, and resources. And they all have problems, weaknesses, and ineptitudes. Are we simply in the habit of looking at kids and focusing primarily on what's wrong? In the case of Elaine, that was easy to do because her glass was even more than half empty. She had abilities and strengths, but not many, and they weren't very apparent at first. It was much easier to see her deficiencies.

Traditionally, in the mental health professions, we like to look at the gap between the water level and the top of the glass. For example, in graduate school, I learned all kinds of neat vocabulary words to describe my clients' unappealing traits and objectionable actions: hypervigilance, anal retentiveness, codependency, dysfunctional family dynamics, borderline personalities, paranoid ideation, and manipulativeness, to name a few. We didn't talk much about courage, heroism, stable personalities, or functional families.

In an objective sense, a problem orientation and a solution orientation may be equally true in any given case. The glass truly is half full *and* half empty. Nonetheless, we choose to attend to one or the other, the fullness or the emptiness. This is not an academic argument. The way we think about and talk about our kids does matter. The case of Elaine clearly demonstrates that. What we look for, we will find, and what we dwell upon, we will perpetuate. We can foster coping and stress resistance by the way we think about and talk with children. And we do it by maintaining a competence orientation. We must talk more about their successes than about their failures. In times of stress, we must help them engage their competence. When their attempts to cope break down, we must look for the resource or skill that is being masked by the symptom. Usually there is a healthy striving under the surface of the problem, which we can miss when the problem itself is so conspicuous.

By celebrating their competence, we teach our kids this competence orientation as well. Hopefully they will follow our lead and remain more focused on their abilities and strengths than on their inadequacies. This may just be the strongest armor that we can give them against adversity and the challenges of life.

YOU ARE HERE

KIDS ARE HERE

PART 2

How to Neutralize Parent Paralyzers

ANYONE WHO SPENDS *time around creatures from beyond the earth's atmosphere runs the risk that it will happen to them. They will be paralyzed. Frozen. Stunned. Petrified. Unable to move. Still living, but temporarily out of commission. No longer able to fend for themselves, let alone take care of those who depend on them.*

It happens to the best of them. Superman was occasionally rendered powerless by kryptonite. Captain Picard was once immobilized by an evil alien probe. You remember when Han Solo was flash-frozen in a slab of carbonite. It was Buck Rogers who was literally frozen for five hundred years. On a trans-polar flight his ship was caught in a blizzard over Alaska and he crashed in the Arctic terrain. As an avalanche covered the wreckage, experimental novano gas flooded his cabin, placing him in a state of suspended animation, where he remained until he was revived centuries later to help free the Hidden City from Killer Kane.

The forces that immobilize us as parents are more subtle. Guilt. Ambiguity. Mistakes. Feelings of inadequacy. Perfectionism. Anxiety. Not quite as scary as novano gas or carbonite, but potentially just as debilitating. Each one can sap our energy and undermine our sense of competence. When parents are immobilized, the primary hazard is to our children. Our effectiveness in addressing their needs is compromised. In a depleted state, we miss important cues and are soft when they need a firm hand or sharp when they need a gentle touch. So, if not for our own good, we need to battle these paralyzers for the sake of our children.

Neutralizing Parent Paralyzer 1: Guilt

In Club Parenthood, there is no trial offer. By the time you fully understand the dues, it's too late to cancel your membership. Guilt, it seems, is one of those things that just comes with the territory, one of the dues you pay for being a parent.

Some parents may have no problem with guilt. When Spider Man and Mary Jane have kids, I'll bet good ol' Spidey will never feel guilty. Being superhuman, he won't make any of the mistakes we mortals make.

The rest of us are less fortunate. Given that mistakes are inevitable, one of the other dues in Club Parenthood is the risk of being criticized for our mistakes and blamed for our kids' problems.

Our children look to us first as the prime movers of their universe. I was reminded of this one day when the ice-cream truck we were chasing rounded the corner and drove out of sight. My two-year-old son, Aaron, looked up at me and, in a matter-of-fact tone, requested, "Bring it back, Dad." Unfortunately, kids aren't the only ones who attribute power of this magnitude to parents. In the view of many professionals, children are mere lumps of clay, parents the mighty sculptors.

During my training in psychology, I was surprised how frequently parents were made the scapegoat. For example, I remember one research article entitled "Child-Rearing Antecedents of

Adult Criminal Behavior." The researchers were looking to answer the age-old question of why bad people do bad things—or perhaps what makes them bad people in the first place. Not surprisingly, the article did find significant differences in the way these criminals had been raised, compared with the rest of the population. Although I found the results interesting, I was puzzled by the very premise of the research. Why were we looking to place the responsibility of people's actions on their parents, especially considering that these criminals were grown-ups now?

Researchers have good intentions, I'm sure. But when they find something wrong with a child or someone who was once a child, they begin searching the immediate vicinity for a suspect to blame. And parents are usually right there.

For quite a while parents were blamed for autism, one of the most serious developmental disorders. Refrigerator mothers, as researchers called them, were so cold and unfeeling that they *caused* children to become autistic. This "discovery" showed up in professional journals and abnormal psychology textbooks a few short decades ago. Needless to say, the "news" was devastating to the mothers of these kids—not only were they faced with raising handicapped children, they were blamed for the handicap. Fortunately, some professionals did not consider the puzzle solved, and subsequent research has demonstrated that autism is genetic. So what about those "refrigerator mothers" we thought were at fault? Well, we've learned that any adult, when interacting with an autistic child who does not respond to communication, tends to disengage emotionally.

So we're not responsible for all our kids' problems. But even when our guilt is well placed—when we're truly not doing all we can as parents—we still have to be careful how we let guilt affect us. Unchecked, guilt can turn us into doormats. We've been working two jobs. We've hardly spent any time with Junior. So even when he spits on the back of his sister's head on the way to McDonald's, we don't want to take away the privilege of playing in the McDonaldland playground after dinner—that would ruin the plan for the night. And it's not like we have many nights like this together. So we let it go. Guilt has just depleted our power.

Guilt may be part of being a parent, but it can balloon out of proportion, sap our energy, and sour our interactions with our kids. So let's be more realistic in the doses of guilt we're willing to swallow. As parents, we're not quite as powerful as we and other people sometimes think we are. And perhaps that's not such a bad thing.

Neutralizing Parent Paralyzer 2: Ambiguity

Each child is different, and each situation we face is complicated by factors beyond our control. So every step of the way, even when we do our best, we are at risk of making mistakes. It seems that parenting is not a science—it's an art. What am I saying? It's not even an art—it's more like a crapshoot! We don't know how things will work out in the end; nonetheless, when a situation comes up we have to place our bet (make a decision) and roll the dice (act on it).

I've heard many people say that raising children is one of the most important functions in our society and yet we require no training at all for the job. They make the point that we need a license to drive a car, a food-handlers permit to cook fast food, even a license to get married. And yet, they complain, anyone can become a parent. Folks making this point are usually arguing that parents should receive training too. They'll get no argument from me on that. But perhaps there's a reason we don't issue parenting permits. The thing is, once I have a driver's license, I know how the car's going to respond when I get behind the wheel. With kids, your guess is as good as mine! I can get all the parent training I want, and it won't prevent me from spending an awful lot of time scratching my head.

A problem has resulted from all these voices promoting more training for parents. Parents question their own competence.

Perhaps that's the idea—maybe then they'll learn more. But if kids are really as creative and mysterious as I think they are, then no amount of training can provide us with clear-cut answers for every situation. Once we think we have them figured out, they almost always throw us something new.

Another problem with listening to experts is that, due to the complexity of raising kids, we hear contradictions from them all the time. In case you haven't heard, here are some of the latest warnings about how you can screw up your children:

• If you feed your kids processed food that has more cholesterol, you place them at risk for heart disease in the future. On the other hand, if you feed them fresh fruits and vegetables, you'll probably give them cancer from pesticides.

• The behaviorists say that if you talk with a child who's upset, you're reinforcing bad behavior. Dr. Spock and the Freudians insist that if you ignore upset children, you're failing to teach them how to talk out their emotions.

• If you're too lenient, your children will be spoiled and have a tough time facing challenges in the real world. If you're too strict, your child will be perfectionistic and have low self-esteem.

Obviously, if we listen to all of the experts, we're left paralyzed—unable to do anything at all! When someone asks, "Did you sleep well last night?" comedian Steven Wright responds, "No. I made a few mistakes." Maybe more than we realize, our actions as parents are like sleeping: our different choices don't always represent right and wrong ways of doing things, simply differences in our style.

I once worked with a single mother who left her son in the care of his grandparents for six hours a day on weekdays so that she could get her training to become a veterinarian. She had worked as a cook for a couple of years to try to pay the bills after her husband left the family, but that didn't provide enough income. She had always wanted to be an animal doctor, so she enrolled in the prestigious but grueling program at the University of California at Davis. She was now in her final year, and she attended the parent support group we offered at the university counseling center. As her son played with the other kids on the rug, she voiced her concerns: Had their bond been damaged? Was she an unfit mother? Had she put him through too much? As we talked, it became apparent that her son had given her no cause for concern. She was simply worried about whether she had done the right thing.

"None of his playmates have to wake up at 6:00 A.M. to go to Grandma and Grandpa's house," she said, offering evidence of the hardship her choices had caused him.

"Maybe not," I responded, "but how many of them get to walk through a real pigsty every Saturday? How many of them have had a peregrine falcon rest on their arm? How many of them have looked through a plastic window to watch a cow's stomach at work?" She smiled as she realized I was right. Perhaps her son was worse off in some ways because of who his mother was. But he was also better off in some other ways.

Sure, we make errors. But perhaps not every action we lose sleep over is an error. There are environments that are harmful for children, and I think kids should be removed from those environments. But I'm convinced that most of us offer our children unique environments that are not necessarily any better or worse than anyplace else they might have landed. For every hole or gap that might lead to our children missing out on something, there may be a strength or resource we offer that more than compensates. Some of us are artistic, some of us are ambitious, some of us are studious, some of us are athletic, some of us are sociable, some of us are easygoing. Our kids will reap both the blessings and the curses of our particular strengths and lifestyles.

So have a little more respect for your own qualities—and for the unique environment and opportunities you provide your kids. Don't let the ambiguity of your job undermine your confidence in your intuition. You—and not some expert—are the best judge of what your kids need. Trust yourself. Raising kids is complicated stuff. Just because you're not always sure you're making the right decision, don't ever assume you're not the right person for the position. Your kids don't need someone who has passed a licensing exam. What they do need are parents who are confident they can do the job.

Neutralizing Parent Paralyzer 3: Mistakes

As a parent, I envy movie directors who can call out "take two" when a scene doesn't go quite as they wanted. In my more neurotic moments, it feels like my mistakes are all captured permanently, every one of them "in the can" and ready to be played like scenes from a poorly scripted movie for the hosts of heaven on judgment day. And it's not just me who will suffer for my blunders. I fear that these mistakes will take on a life of their own that continues even after I am dead and gone. I will be a case study in some future edition of the book *Toxic Parents*. That will be my legacy. Generations from now, my family line will remain polluted by my stupid choices.

Even though we cannot edit out the parts we don't like from our interactions with our kids, fortunately we do get plenty of chances to apologize, ask for forgiveness, and try to do better. We can call out "take two" and try a scene again, even though that may not erase the mess we made of it the first time. I was grateful for this fact one day not long ago when I goofed up big time.

I confiscated the snack my son had brought to school. It wasn't so much what I did, though, as the way I did it. I raised my voice and was stern with him when gentle firmness would have been the ticket. I got my way, but I saw that he was in tears as he walked through the front door of the school.

Sitting in the car with the little guy's three Fig Newtons, I felt like a big, mean bully. To top it off, when I got back home, my wife, Jenny, confirmed that Ryan had told me the truth. "I'm pretty sure it is okay with his teacher if they eat snacks during their afternoon rest time."

My initial impulse was to defend myself. So I did. *How was I to know snacks were okay!?! I could never take snacks to school as a kid! I figured the other kids would feel left out! And what about the custodian—cleaning up crumbs every day. Doesn't anyone besides me think of the poor custodian!?!*

When I calmed down enough to see past my own ego, I knew what I had to do. I put four Fig Newtons in a little brown paper bag and returned to Layton Elementary. With my tail between my legs, I walked into classroom 18. "Okay if I drop off some snacks for my son?" I asked Ms. Coy. "Fine. They're just first graders," she reminded me. "I give 'em a break midafternoon." *And I should give one more often too,* I thought. I delivered the bag to my son, who grinned back at me. "Thanks, Dad." "I'm sorry I didn't believe you," I said as I gave him a hug.

"Is that your dad?" one of his classmates asked as I was leaving. I looked back to see Ryan nod his head as he opened the bag to show his friend its contents.

As I left the classroom and walked down the hall, I could feel the spring return to my step. The knot in my stomach was beginning to loosen. *That was more like it,* I thought as I walked from the building to my car. *Take two is a wrap!*

NEUTRALIZING PARENT PARALYZER 4: FEELINGS OF INADEQUACY

Parents need not feel capable all the time in order to succeed. In fact, there will be times when we'll feel useless. Again and again, raising children will frustrate us and make us feel incapable. It's one of the things kids do best. If you feel frustrated and inadequate most of the time, maybe you need to get help; if you feel frustrated and inadequate frequently, welcome to Club Parenthood.

I believe that being a parent is one of the most difficult tasks in the world, in part because it constantly brings our powerlessness into our view. And into plain view of everyone standing behind us in line at the grocery store . . . and the library . . . and the bank (thank goodness for automatic tellers).

Complete control over children is only possible through the use of regular force and violence. Every now and then I read a newspaper story about a father or mother who has killed his or her own child because the child wouldn't stop crying. The parent usually assumes, "If I were a good enough parent, I could do the right thing and the baby would calm down." They fail to realize that there may be nothing they can do to soothe the child for the time being. And so they interpret the crying as a message they're not good enough as parents. Perhaps they could tolerate the noise itself, but they find the feelings of inadequacy intolerable. Eventually their frustration turns to anger.

Maybe these parents are under the mistaken impression that there are people who *don't* have times when they feel useless with their kids, who can always get them to stop crying. But it's not true with infants, and it's not true with older kids either. We can do a decent job as parents and still feel useless at times. Sometimes success as a parent may mean simply choosing not to abuse your children even when they make you feel incapable.

I used to work at Utah Youth Village, a residential treatment program with therapeutic group homes and foster homes. One day I talked on the phone with a mother who had just sent her daughter from out of state into one of our group homes. I could tell right away she had been overwhelmed by advice on how to be a better parent.

"I admit it, I'm a wimp," she confessed. "I've been to all kinds of professionals and they teach me how to be a better parent, but when it comes to applying the principles, I blow it. I can't enforce anything right."

She didn't complain once about her child's behavior, just about her own failures and weaknesses.

The next day I sat down in therapy to talk to her fifteen-year-old daughter. "You can try to work with my mom, but she's heard it all before. She knows what to do, she just can't do it. Here's what I mean: One day I get home from school and decide to go driving. [She didn't have permission or a driver's license.] Well, I take off and go pick up my friends and we go cruising. I stay out until midnight, and on my way home, going around this turn on the road to our house, I cream the side of the car against the guardrail. I get home, and Mom sees the entire side of the car smashed in. Do you know what she says? 'Go to bed. Think about what your punishment should be, and we'll deal with it in the morning.' Can you believe she did that? '*You* think about what your punishment should be. We'll deal with it in the morning'!"

Just like her mother, this girl placed very little emphasis on her own behavior; she talked only about her mom's failures and weaknesses.

My message to both of them was: "Mom is doing fine. Daughter needs to change. Mom will never be locked up or sent to a treatment program for the way she's being a parent. Daughter has been locked up and is in a treatment program for the way she's being as a kid."

Daughter: "That's messed up. So it's all me? I have to do all the changing?"

Answer: "Not if you like being in a treatment program!"

Judging her own skills had focused this mother on herself—on her own reprehensible, pathetic performance. Tons of advice and the difficulty of her task as a parent had turned her judgment inward, on what she was doing wrong, on how she was falling short.

When we recognize that we're focused more on our own performance than on our kids' needs and welfare, we should turn our attention back to our children and demand better of them. If we think we need to be perfect parents before we can require our kids to measure up to some standard of expectation, we—and they—are going to be in trouble.

Neutralizing Parent Paralyzer 5: Perfectionism

Nothing means more to me than my family," a woman said to me recently. "I just wish I could be a perfect mother."

If I were a genie and this mother had just summoned me from my lamp, I'd try to talk her out of that wish. After all, if she were perfect, her children would grow up to be weak and helpless. If she met all of her kids' needs, how would they ever learn to delay gratification? If her kids never had to struggle because of her goof-ups, how would they get along in a world full of real people?

Having perfect parents would be a curse. Having had everything provided for us in the past, we'd have no clue how to meet our own needs and take care of ourselves.

Imagine the son of a perfect mother, twenty years down the road, looking for a wife. "I can find someone who will meet all of my needs. Nothing less than perfection will do. I know that women like this exist; I just have to find someone like my mother."

When we mess up and make mistakes, our kids not only become stronger and more self-sufficient, they learn vital survival skills like apologizing and forgiving. On the other hand, parents who are satisfied with nothing less than perfection in themselves don't raise perfect kids—they raise neurotic ones.

Little Rosie watches her mom toil and sweat to "get everything done." She hears Mom berate herself for forgetting the PTA meeting because she was so busy. She sees Mom distraught and apologetic because "the house is a mess" when a neighbor drops by. What does all this teach Rosie about missing a problem on a math assignment or dropping the ball during a Little League game?

Since it's truly impossible to do the job of raising kids without committing some errors, perfectionistic parents may end up denying their mistakes in order to avoid feeling guilty. "I've done everything I could to be a good parent" really means, "I'm afraid to admit that sometimes I mess up." Maybe they hope that if they talk about everything they've done right, no one will see their blunders.

But when we deny our faults as parents, we can really irritate our kids. I know it may sound far-fetched, but my observation of families has convinced me that nothing pushes rebellious kids further in the direction of more mistakes than having parents who won't admit they've made some mistakes themselves. When troubled kids see their parents pretending they're only sugar and spice and everything nice, it's as though they go to the other extreme to provide some balance.

When a parent won't admit shortcomings, someone else must shoulder all the blame for problems. The other parent or one of the children often bears that burden. "It's hell because of Kathy. Ever since she was thirteen, our lives have been miserable. If it weren't for her, our family would be getting along just fine. In fact, Susan and I have even been having problems in our marriage lately—see what having a difficult teenager does to the rest of the family?"

Yeah, right. Kathy may have made some mistakes, but is she really powerful enough to drag down your marriage?

Problems and errors are inevitable; how we handle them is up to us. We can be critical of ourselves or our children, or we can see our mistakes as opportunities to learn and grow. We have the chance to show our kids that relationships can survive mistakes and outlive conflict. By example we can teach them how to laugh at themselves and accept their own frailties. And these skills will serve them much better than the memory of a flawless mother and the unquenchable yearning for someone perfect to take her place.

Neutralizing Parent Paralyzer 6:
Anxiety

We try to do what's best for our children, but let's be honest: Sometimes our responses are not well thought out. They are of the knee-jerk variety.

Knee-jerk responses are particularly likely when our kids push our buttons. Their actions trigger an emotion in us, and that emotion short-circuits our brain and determines our response. In other words, our own hang-ups get in the way of our doing what's best for our kids.

Next time you have a hard time with your kids, ask yourself if perhaps your anxiety has been triggered and is keeping you from handling the situation more effectively.

Take the case of Stacy, for example. She had been abused by her own father. He had slapped her face and spanked her with a belt when she was younger, and had humiliated her in front of her friends when she was a teenager. As an adult, she felt anger welling up inside her whenever she thought about him. She had vowed long ago never to be like him with her own kids.

Raising her first two children seemed like a piece of cake. Her daughters responded very well to her gentle persuasion and felt guilty at the very mention of her displeasure. They were very well-behaved young ladies.

But her third child, a boy, was now three years old, and he was a terror. Derrick didn't do what she asked—no matter how nicely she asked. He was out of control at home, in the neighbor-hood, and at church. He left destruction in his wake everywhere he went.

Everywhere except at Stacy's father's house! Grandpa was very firm with him, and Derrick seemed to respect that authority—or maybe he just feared it. And he did have a preschool teacher who was pretty strict and seemed to bring him under control.

Stacy had asked her children's pediatrician for help. The doc-tor said Stacy was letting Derrick walk all over her, and she needed to be more firm with him. For a few weeks Stacy tried, but her efforts just didn't seem to make a difference. Eventually the doc-tor reluctantly prescribed some Ritalin to see if that would calm the child down.

Stacy came in to me for counseling to see if there was more we could do for Derrick's "hyperactivity." As I assessed the boy, I found he didn't fit the diagnostic criteria for Attention Deficit Disorder. So I watched him and Mom together. I noticed how she hesitated to discipline him. She told me about how harsh her father was, and how she had promised herself she would be dif-ferent. But now she had a dilemma. Her son didn't respond to her gentle approach.

She knew she had to be more firm with him—and if she had a moment of doubt about that, everyone from her doctor to her neighbors to the cashier at the grocery store was reminding her it was true. Problem was, she couldn't bring herself to do it.

As she and I worked together, Stacy began to recognize that even moving in the direction of firmness triggered an anxious feel-ing inside. Her own experience with her father was a trauma that remained alive in her heart. All of the helplessness and fear and anger of that trauma had created a sort of wall of anxiety, which acted as a barrier to more effective discipline.

So Stacy had to practice firm discipline, even when doing so meant dredging up again a taste of that terror and pain from yes-teryear. Interestingly, in the process she gained new insights about her own relationship with her dad and developed a deeper respect for her own resilience. This new perspective gave her even more confidence as a parent. She was still different from her father—she wasn't abusive. But now she was no longer driven to be "soft." She could choose her response and act in her son's best interest. She was usually her gentle, loving, supportive old self, but at times she could be a strict, loving, demanding new self.

The difference for Stacy occurred when she took the courage to stay in charge even when she felt uneasy about it. Her attempts to take charge triggered anxiety, but she stayed the course. Courage is the essence of effective child-rearing. Doing what is best for our kids can sometimes be a daunting task—and that is when wimps bail out instead of taking the heat. We have to be willing to ride out the discomfort when we know we're acting for the good of our children.

Remember That Course Corrections Are Part of the Journey

When Stanley shot a neighbor boy in the behind with his BB gun, his parents were alarmed. I know because I lived just up the street from Stanley. He was a great friend. We had a lot of fun together, Stanley and I. But not during the month after this incident. That's because he was spending every minute of what would have been his free time at home doing heavy labor as a punishment for what he had done.

At the time, some people who knew Stanley may have been worried about what he would become. But guess what—he turned out just fine! In fact, he is a hardworking, highly successful engineer, a decent citizen, and a conscientious father. If any of his sons ever shoot a neighbor in the behind with their BB gun, they will probably be doing hard labor for two months.

I want to be clear here: I don't mean to downplay the seriousness of violence by children. We have all seen just how dangerous kids with guns can be. I relay this story simply because it was something that happened in my neighborhood, so I have witnessed firsthand what has transpired in the intervening twenty years. It stands out to me as a troubling incident that was *not* a signal of future problems. In this era when we are being inundated with lists of danger signals and warning signs, it is important to remember that kids can do some pretty alarming things on their way to becoming perfectly well-adjusted adults. That should give us permission to relax and enjoy the sometimes bumpy ride.

In his book *The Seven Habits of Highly Effective Families,* Stephen Covey points out that even good families may spend most of their time off course. But as parents we can be like airline pilots, who also spend the better part of a flight off course, yet constantly adjust their flight plans to take into account errors they have made so far. If we continue to make course corrections, we can arrive at our destination despite all the time we spent off course along the way.

Let's say I have been too strict as a parent. Even if I have, all is not lost. I will lighten up a little, observe how my kids respond, and then adjust course again when I get more feedback. For me, that's the easy part: Jenny and the boys are always willing to give me more feedback! But what if I err in the other direction, becoming too lenient? That will become apparent soon enough, and I'll keep working to strike a good balance, to find that happy medium.

Our kids will mess up, and we will too. As long as we remember where we want to go and keep comparing that with where we are headed, we can make the necessary course corrections. A month of heavy labor can be a good course correction for an errant son. An anger-management class can be just as helpful for Mom or Dad. We should be proud of, not embarrassed over, that kind of course correction.

YOU ARE HERE

KIDS ARE HERE

PART 3

Tricks of the Trade for Jovian Trainers

(HECKING OUT THE WORK *of other psychologists, I've seen some pretty incredible things. I've seen pigeons play table tennis. I've seen a bear ride a motorcycle. I've seen gerbils that water-ski—and one that could even parasail! The one that amazed me most was the pig that did the shopping. (Okay, so it couldn't write out the check at the checkout line, but it was able to push the shopping cart around.)*

If these creatures can be trained to do such amazing feats, why can't we get a teenager to lift up the toilet seat? Why do we have such a hard time getting a two-year-old to wear a bib? Part of it is that Jovians are a lot smarter, more complex creatures than pigeons, bears, gerbils, or pigs. Our efforts are also complicated by the fact that at the same time we are trying to train them, they are also working to train us!

However, just as circus trainers and psychologists have figured out some of the tricks to training other species from this planet, there are some principles we can apply as we attempt to influence our little friends from Jupiter.

Increase Your Influence by Building Connection

The most successful attempts to influence are those built upon the foundation of a strong, connected relationship. Influence that relies upon power or authority has much less chance of success. Coercion may appear to work for a time, but it always breaks down in the long run.

Society will probably never be able to control some of the prison inmates with whom I have worked. They feel little or no connection to other people, and hence they are not open to social influence. There's a lesson in that: If we wish to stay in charge of our children, we must build and maintain our relationships with them.

As I talk with groups of parents, I ask those who have more than one child to raise their hands if there is one in particular to whom they feel the least connected. Almost all of them raise their hands. Then I ask them to raise their hands if that child is also the reason they are attending a workshop on discipline techniques. Again, almost all of them raise their hands. This is not a coincidence. Part of it may be that our relationship with children deteriorates as they defy us and resist our authority. But I don't think that's the whole story. I think that when there's a lack of connection to begin with, we have a more difficult time convincing children to do what we know is best for them.

Our bond with our children is not simply a tool of influence. It can become a tremendous resource, a reservoir from which they can draw future strength in times of need.

There are several things we can do that will help us truly get to know our children and develop the kind of bond that will strengthen them and make them more receptive to our influence. First, we must open ourselves up to our children and to the realities of our relationships. This means that we must risk the possibility that our preconceptions about a child may be shattered. "There is nothing more thrilling in this world, I think, than having a child that is yours, and yet is mysteriously a stranger." I think it's fitting that Agatha Christie, the British suspense novelist, made that statement about the element of mystery that exists in even this closest of relationships.

We have to be willing to allow our view of our children to evolve. Kids are like the proverbial river that we can never set foot in twice. We have had certain experiences with them, and have created mental models of our children based on those interactions and observations. The problem is, whereas our model may remain static, our children are constantly changing, becoming new and different people, at least in little ways, every day. So we need to observe, to commit ourselves to pay attention. That's connection. It's very different from the psychological violence of keeping a child pigeonholed.

I used to have a fairly knee-jerk response to my kids' tantrums or anger outbursts. I would always to try to contain such explosions as soon as possible and inform the offending child that his behavior was not acceptable. Such turmoil made me uncomfortable, and I reacted with a little turmoil of my own. I was fighting fire with fire. With a little prompting from Jenny, however, I am now more often able to take deep breaths in an effort to remain calm, and observe my children instead. "What happened just before he got upset?" "What do I know about my child's personality that would make sense of this behavior?" "Is this outburst an indication of fatigue? Desperation? Frustration? Feelings of helplessness? Anger?"

As I've taken a step back and become more observant in this way, I have gotten to know my kids better. I'm more aware, for example, that Aaron wants to be bigger than he is. Many of his tantrums occur when he's not included in something because of his size or age. So now I make an effort to include him in the kinds of "grown-up" activities he can handle. Perhaps as a result, he gets frustrated less frequently now.

Ryan, on the other hand, seems to become particularly upset when something violates his expectations or disrupts the patterns and routines to which he is accustomed. I can bypass some tantrums by making sure I talk him through changes I know will be difficult. "I know it's hard to leave your friends, but in five minutes we're going in the car to pick up Mom."

As we get to know our kids better, we can do more to facilitate their growth and development. For me this has meant becoming more flexible, instead of reacting to all tantrums with the cookie-cutter response: "I don't have to tolerate this." But there's no way of predicting what kind of changes such knowledge will lead to for you and your family. That mystery is for you alone to investigate.

In one workshop I taught, a father was talking about how his daughter was not a *bad* kid, she just wasn't becoming the kind of young adult he had anticipated. A couple of minutes into his mourning the loss of the daughter he had fantasized about raising, one of the other participants spoke up. "It sounds to me like you planned a trip to France and you ended up in Holland. Don't let the fact that you're not in Paris blind you to the beauty that Holland has to offer." That's good advice to all parents.

As you seek to deepen your relationship with your child, remember that the investment of energy and time together is far more important than the nature of the activity being shared. I once worked with Tony, a sixteen-year-old who was in treatment for drug addiction. Tony had been living with his mother, but when the police found marijuana and drug paraphernalia in the back of his Jeep, he was arrested and sent to jail. Following his release, it was determined that perhaps he needed more of his father's influence, and he was sent to live with him.

Tony's father had not been very involved in his children's lives since the divorce. But he felt a responsibility to help his son now, and he accepted the obligation of having Tony come to live with him.

Of course, there were a lot of issues to work through. On Tony's part, resentment and anger had built up over the years as he had witnessed his father's apparent lack of interest in the family. Dad had moved on, it seemed to Tony, to his second wife's family, leaving his own family in the dust. Dad felt guilty but also angry that he didn't get more credit for the effort he did make, given the bitter divorce and his busy life.

Over time, I watched Tony's relationship with his dad become the most important ingredient in his recovery program. As an outside observer, I was interested to note their contrasting perceptions of what Dad was now doing that made him an effective father. Dad thought he was handling problems in the right way because he had learned some of the theory regarding drug addiction. He considered himself effective as a disciplinarian when Tony broke the rules. He felt like he must be communicating well and saying the right kinds of things when they talked. When I talked to Tony, however, it became clear that it wasn't the specific things his dad had learned or said or done that made the difference—it was simply that now Dad *was* learning and saying and doing. He was spending time and energy being with and finding out about his son.

One of the things they enjoyed doing together was working on motorcycles. When Tony completed the intensive portion of his drug-treatment program, the other group members asked him what would motivate him to stay clean. I thought he made a pretty good case. "I have too much to look forward to," he said. "I have work, I have the chance to move out on my own next year, I don't want to waste my life. Besides, I can finally run down the basketball court without collapsing, like I used to. This summer my dad and I are going cross-country on our bikes. You have to be 'with it' on the road. I would never throw that all away for a chance to get high with my buddies again."

An atmosphere that is warm and welcoming can help set the stage for connection. I heard one father, LeGrand Curtis, say that "ice cream is better bought early than wished for later," meaning that he would rather have his kids and their friends searching the refrigerator at home than cruising around somewhere else. When your kids and their friends enjoy being around you, you will have more opportunities to discover who they are and influence them for good.

As you build your relationship with your children, be careful not to push so hard to connect that you drive them away. Teenagers, in particular, value their independence. They cherish their free time and private space, so be realistic and reasonable in the time you expect to spend together as a family. You might invite them to bring a friend to family activities—perhaps even on family trips—if that would encourage attendance and improve morale.

Emotionally, kids feel tension in two directions at once. In a way, security in family relationships prepares them for independence, so don't be surprised if just when you're feeling especially close, they push you away and want their space. Don't worry, they'll be back. Stay constant in your love and support, and the connection they have with you will be like an emotional anchor. They'll need it when the waters get rough.

Pounce When Your Children Are Behaving

Rats learn to press levers and pigeons learn to turn circles if they are reinforced or rewarded following those behaviors. Similarly, behavior is often maintained by children because it is being reinforced in some way. However, reinforcement does not occur only when we *try* to reward a child. Sometimes, our reinforcement of behavior is inadvertent. The attention a child receives when he or she is scolded, for instance, may be enough to reinforce the behavior.

Perhaps we've all known someone who watches and waits for something to go wrong, and then pounces on that problem as evidence that they "just can't win" and "things are hopeless." No matter how many good things happen, it's as though only the problems and crises register.

With kids, this approach can be disastrous. When we constantly pounce only on bad behavior, our kids may be getting what is called "bootleg reinforcement." Even though we don't mean to encourage their misdeeds, kids often repeat whatever brings them the most attention.

We all spend time and effort identifying what's wrong and trying to root out the problems. But it really is possible—and often more effective—to improve things by dwelling on the good events that happen. Every child engages in a wide range of behavior. So the children we'd like to guide are probably already doing what we want them to do—at times. We have to pay careful attention and try to "catch 'em being good." Amazingly, when we are vigilant in our search for what's right, and pounce when we see something good, we will likely discover there's just as much to celebrate in our children's behavior as there is to curse. Maybe even more!

When Ryan, our eldest child, was three, and his brother, Aaron, was one, they had already begun their rivalry. Being very mature and restrained for his age, Aaron would patiently wait for his brother to choose a toy. Then he'd decide that was just the one he wanted. No, *needed*. Desperately. *Right now!* Always the magnanimous older brother, Ryan quickly learned to exploit every such opportunity to engage in a little taunting and psychological torture.

One Sunday afternoon as I watched them play on the kitchen floor, I saw what looked like the same old pattern emerging. Ryan was playing with his Tonka trucks, and Aaron crawled over and tried to get involved. Ryan held his hand out to stop him, but Aaron persisted. Ryan then gave Aaron a little shove, and Aaron squealed in frustration.

Ordinarily I would have stepped in at that point, saying something authoritative like, "Play nicely together." If I had been feeling very energetic, or perhaps if blood had been drawn, I might have resorted to time-out. But this time I decided to just wait. I wanted to see if there would eventually be something positive I could pounce on.

For a while, I doubted it would happen. Aaron continued his pursuit, and Ryan persisted in fending him off, and the squealing continued. To my surprise, however, after a couple of minutes the struggle ended. I looked down and saw that Aaron had his hands on Ryan's big yellow tractor. Ryan was playing with his dump truck and didn't seem bothered by his brother's presence.

That was when I pounced.

"You guys are playing together so well. Ryan, thanks for letting Aaron play with your tractor—look at how happy he is. You're sharing."

Ryan looked up and then went on playing. I had no idea of the impact of what I had done until later that evening. Ryan, who was eating dried fruit snacks out of a bag, walked up to Aaron and popped one in his mouth. "I share you, Aar-Bear," he said. "You yike dat?"

Chills ran down my spine as I realized my power. A simple comment from Dad had stayed with him for hours! If that was all it took, what misbehavior had I been encouraging inadvertently by commenting on it? For better or worse, my son was keeping track of what I noticed and talked about.

We do have this kind of power. Our kids do keep track. And our comments and actions register even in ways we don't intend. So sit back for a change. Watch your kids. Wait patiently. And when you see something good . . . *pounce!*

Entice Them Instead of Forcing Them

It was bedtime, and I wanted to get the kids to read books so that we could all wind down. Ryan was playing with a truck at the foot of his bed, and Aaron was busy working all four of the hippos on his "Hungry Hungry Hippos" game. Using my most enthusiastic sales pitch, I told both of them to put away their toys and come up on the bed to read.

"I've got *The Cat in the Hat* and *Babar!*"

No response.

I would have raised my voice a few decibels and tried to adopt a more commanding tone, but I was tired. I didn't have the energy to force the issue, so I lay down on one of their beds. On a whim, I opened up *The Cat in the Hat* and started reading softly to myself.

Before I was done with the second page, the hippos had stopped eating marbles. Aaron stood next to the bed, craning his neck to see the picture. He soon climbed up and nuzzled next to me for story time.

Ryan resisted the temptation a bit longer. But he loves Thing One and Thing Two, and when we got to that part of the story, he climbed up on the bed and crowded right in.

That night, I was reminded that enticement usually works better than force. As parents, we don't have to make everything work out. Sometimes we can make requests and then, if our kids don't respond, simply remind them what they will be missing if they continue. It may be nothing more than a story. It may be

some privilege. Or it may be something tangible, one of the goodies they enjoy on a daily basis.

When they learn about the idea of enticing kids, some parents
think, "Great, now I have to buy more stuff for my kids if I want
them to mind." Not so. When it comes to enticing our kids, we
tend to overlook all of the good things we already provide. We
assume our children deserve everything we can give them. And
our kids catch on; they feel entitled to whatever they get. But
they're not! Much of what we give our kids is above and beyond
the call of parental duty. We can best prepare kids for life by
requiring that they contribute in return for some of what they get.

Look at the following list. Ask yourself, in your home, are
these items goodies that must be earned or entitlements every
child deserves?

- TV
- Three square meals a day
- Stories at bedtime
- Radio, cassette, or CD player
- Nintendo
- A roof overhead
- Playtime with friends
- Enjoyable family activities
- Dessert
- Toys to play with

There are certain things every child should have: a safe place
to live, a healthy diet, a comfortable home. Jenny and I have also
decided that in our home no child will ever be left out of a family
activity. The other items listed are nice luxuries, but kids don't
really need them—no matter how vehemently they insist they do.

It can actually be quite easy to entice kids. Consider this
simple example of following "Grandma's Rule," which dictates that
the chores come before the fun. One afternoon our family was

planning to carve pumpkins for Halloween. We also had to clean up the house. We told Ryan and Aaron, "As soon as we've cleaned all the bedrooms, we'll carve the pumpkins." We were amazed how hard a four- and two-year-old could work when they knew we were going to get to do something fun when they got finished. Jenny and I knew from experience that they wouldn't have cooperated nearly as well had we carved the pumpkins first and *then* tried to get them to help clean up.

Ride Out Extinction Bursts

The term *extinction* has been applied by psychologists to the phenomenon of reversing the learning process. With the rats that press levers for food pellets and the pigeons that turn circles for birdseed, scientists have discovered that if that reinforcement stops, eventually the behavior will too.

To reduce the occurrence of a behavior that has been reinforced, it's necessary for that behavior to undergo extinction. When reinforcement is no longer forthcoming, animals learn very quickly that their efforts are not rewarded, and they no longer repeat the behavior patterns. Previously reinforced behavior is bound to occur, but the researchers simply provide no reinforcement when it does. The motivation to engage in the behavior is thus undermined, and soon the behavior will disappear completely.

At least, that's the way it's supposed to work. However, in some cases animal researchers observed something interesting when they attempted to stop circle-turning or lever-pressing behavior. They found that sometimes the animal continued the behavior for a short time—almost as though it was testing to see if the reward might perhaps reappear. In fact, an odd thing happened in some cases: an animal would engage in the previously reinforced behavior with even more gusto for a time after the reinforcement had been cut off. "Wait a minute," we can imagine the pigeon thinking, "this was working before. Maybe if I just keep at it long and hard enough . . ." But animals will not maintain such behavior for long without some reward. Following a brief increase, in the end the behavior underwent extinction just as expected. Researchers gave the name *extinction burst* to this phenomenon—a brief escalation of behavior after it is no longer being reinforced.

I was surely glad I knew about extinction bursts when Stella came to see me about her eleven-year-old boy, Evan. Evan was the youngest of four children, and the one with whom Stella had developed the closest bond. They loved hanging out together and had always been able to solve their difficulties by talking them out, but now there was a situation that had become problematic. Evan had been missing more and more school lately. He would leave in the morning feeling fine, but then in the middle of the day Stella would get a call from the school nurse's office. Evan was complaining of a stomachache or a headache. He wanted her to come pick him up and bring him home. Of course, initially Stella was concerned about Evan's health. Following several weeks of a gradual increase in the number of these sick days, she took him to the hospital to be evaluated. They worked him over and could find nothing of concern physically. Because his symptoms seemed to be a way for Evan to get out of school, and because he never felt sick on Saturday or Sunday, the folks at the hospital referred Stella and Evan to the psychology clinic where I worked.

I taught Stella about the principles of reinforcement and extinction. She agreed to try an experiment. We talked with Evan's teacher and the school nurse, who both thought it was worth a try as well. For the next three weeks, when Evan called home, she would express her sympathy over the phone and then inform him that he could stay at the nurse's office until he felt well enough to return to class. If he complained of sickness in the morning before leaving for school, he was to remain in bed throughout that day and evening.

With this new plan in hand, Stella was optimistic. As we were wrapping up our session, I warned her: "Things may get worse before they get better." I explained about the likelihood of an extinction burst, given how consistently Evan's complaints of sickness had been reinforced before. Two days later, Stella called my office. "It was a good thing you warned me," she said. "Evan called this morning complaining of a stomachache. He pouted a bit when I told him the nurse would take care of him there, but after we hung up I thought he had accepted it pretty well. However, after lunch I got another call from him, and he was still in her office. He was in tears, complaining that he couldn't stand the pain. The nurse assured me that she had given him some painkillers and that Evan had declined the opportunity to go see a doctor, but if I hadn't been expecting that extinction burst, that call probably would have put me over the edge. I would have given in and gone to pick him up."

The following week, Evan spent the better part of two days in the nurse's office. On Monday of the third week, Evan stayed home sick. Tuesday morning, he was sick again. By noon, however, he informed Stella that he was feeling well enough to go to school. "Does this mean I can play with Sean this afternoon?" Evan asked Stella as she dropped him off at school. "Absolutely," Stella assured him. That Thursday, Evan spent a half hour in the nurse's office with his final headache of the year. He was still occasionally troubled by stomachaches, particularly when he got nervous, but nothing that kept him out of class for more than an hour or two.

One warning is in order before we end our discussion of this topic. In Evan's case, I was comfortable ignoring one form of communication (his complaints of sickness) because I knew that he and his mother had daily dialogues about his thoughts and feelings, his triumphs and struggles. However, looking back now, I recognize that it would also have been helpful to teach Evan about the effects emotions can have on the body. Specifically, they often trigger physical responses that can mimic actual illness. Let's say Evan's anxiety was triggered when he felt left out of a social group or worked on math concepts that challenged him. When he called home, Stella could have encouraged him to return to class and face the fear, and then spent more time that evening with him talking about how to make friends or drilling math facts.

Whatever tactic you try in an attempt to guide your child, make sure you also keep the lines of communication open, be as perceptive as you can, and then trust your intuition about what's best for your son or daughter.

Try a Spoonful of Sugar

There's an element of fun in every job to be done. At least, Mary Poppins insists there is. And she gets a lot of mileage out of that philosophy. But, then again, Mary Poppins is not working with teenagers.

Turning chores into a game can work wonders with younger kids. One winter day I told my kids how bad I felt that I had no Alaskan Huskies. I needed some good sled dogs to help me clear off the driveway. Good sled dogs, I explained, could help me by pulling loads of snow and ice onto the grass using our toboggan. I even had some dog biscuits (graham crackers) to feed my team. "We can be your dogs, Dad!" they cried. I've never seen such eager beasts of burden.

When my brothers and I made an especially big mess as kids, my mom used to call "Twenty-pick-up!" In this game, the first to put away twenty toys was the winner. Most of the time, the mess was gone before any of us got to twenty.

Soft toys can be tossed into buckets in a game of "basketball." Kids can have races getting their pajamas on. Something as simple as colored toothpicks or decorative cake sprinkles can turn even reluctant kids into kitchen helpers.

Watch your children play and you'll learn what interests them the most. For a child who loves cars, a request for "help driving to the grocery store" will not go unheeded. Hand the child a kitchen plate and encourage him or her to use it to steer the car at the right times. Kids love to pretend to be doctors, nurses, garbage collectors, builders, bakers, and even maids if you reward them with a small "tip" now and then.

Turning work into fun is more difficult with older kids. They usually see right through such propaganda. Humor can work, although probably not as well or as often as it does with their little brothers or sisters. And it must be more skillfully applied—it has to be on their level.

Growing up, I always complained when my mom asked me to do housework. Breaking my stride during a busy day to vacuum? What was she thinking? I'd groan and mumble.

But Mom's comeback disarmed me. "You spend hours every week lifting weights. Think of housework as exercise." That was sure to give me a good laugh, which usually lasted longer than the job I had to do. I'd do curls with the duster as I walked between shelves. I'd grunt and wipe away imaginary sweat as I vacuumed.

When my dad woke us up on Saturday mornings to do chores, he applied the same principle. He would come into our rooms laughing and joking. He'd put our favorite music in the tape player and crank it up, singing the wrong words and dancing to the beat.

To us kids, on the other hand, sleeping in on the weekend was serious business. We would put our pillows over our heads, plead our case, or yell "get out of here!" in as dour a voice as we could manage. But he continued his routine just the same. And we discovered it was impossible to stay angry at such a goofball. On occasion, when I stubbornly remained in bed, he even doused me with water. If he had done it in anger or frustration, I could have self-righteously played the oppressed-child role. But when he was having so much fun, I was at his mercy. Not to be a spoil-sport, I put up with it. And before long, I was out of bed helping him work around the house.

To entertain myself as I worked, I was planning my revenge.

Turnabout is fair play. So what could he do when I stood at the foot of his bed at 6:00 the next morning, with a smile on my face and a Bible in my hand, preaching to him about the evils of slothfulness and indolence?

Redirect Problem Behavior

When children's actions don't make sense, one helpful response is to look beyond the behavior and consider their goal. Kids sometimes use pretty crude and ineffective methods to try to get what they want. It's often easier to help them find a different way to reach their goal than it is to stop their behavior cold.

Several years ago, I had an experience that showed me the power of redirection. I was out in front of our apartment tending eighteen-month-old Ryan. He stood on the sidewalk chatting gibberish and playing with our six-year-old neighbor, Marta.

After awhile, ten-year-old Hector began entertaining himself by "buzzing" the two kids on his bicycle. Obviously delighted by Marta's squeals as he zoomed by, Hector circled the apartment building faster and faster for each pass.

I was getting a little worried about Ryan. He still had the habit of being somewhat oblivious at times to his surroundings, and I wasn't at all sure he wouldn't step into Hector's path. Marta was also clearly worried, and between squeals was lecturing Hector—all to no avail, of course.

My initial intention was to scold him and send him away. Given Marta's lack of success, however, I decided on a different strategy. On his next trip around, I stopped Hector.

"You're going pretty fast."

Hector nodded.

"Can you guess how long it took you to get around the building this last time? Twenty-three seconds. I timed you. How long do you think it would take you to go all the way around the apartment complex?"

Hector shrugged.

"Can you do it in three minutes? Let's see if you can. Five-four-three-two-one-go!"

Hector was off.

Ryan and Marta played about twenty minutes longer, and then we went inside. Later I asked Hector what had happened. He told me that he had found some of his older friends and decided to play with them instead.

My guess is that Hector was bored. He had seized the first entertainment option available. But he was willing to redirect his energy once he saw another possibility.

Even when kids' methods are misguided, their goals are usually quite reasonable. It's up to us to discover their good intentions and help them find better routes to their goals.

Exploit Their Self-Esteem

I hate to use the word *exploit* when talking about strategies for staying in charge. Okay, that's not true—I love it. The word implies that parents can be the conniving ones for a change. It conveys the use of strategy and manipulation—the careful planning of events for effect. And on occasion, every parent ought to carefully orchestrate events for the benefit of a child.

All kids have a drive to be competent and in control. Rather than constantly fighting that need, we parents ought to accept it. And beyond accepting it, we can even use it to our advantage, and to the advantage of our kids.

I recall my father using this technique on me. I didn't resent it a bit. In fact, I've always appreciated the added self-confidence it gave me. One day I was sweeping out the pop-up tent-trailer our family took on camping trips. I didn't want to be there, and Dad probably picked up my signals to that effect. (You know how subtle the sighs and moans of a disgruntled teenager can be.) "Mark," he said, "there's a reason I've asked you to help me clean up. I like how thorough you are. I know if I want something done well, I can count on you to do it just the way I would do it myself."

I probably didn't let on then, but that comment meant a lot to me—obviously, it has stayed with me to this day. I respected my dad and knew how thorough he was. After all, he was a test engineer for a company that built defense systems for the military. His

company trusted that no problems would make it past him unde-
tected.

After that comment, instead of resenting every minute of it, I
probably spent only about 90 percent of my time resenting the
work he assigned me to do. At least 10 percent of the time, I was
taking pride in my efforts. I recall that his description of me as
"thorough" came back to me again and again later. Once, for
example, as I was mowing the lawn, it prompted me to make sure
I mowed right to the edge of the cement wall that divided our yard
from the neighbor's.

In the late 1950s, psychologist Leon Festinger proposed an
idea that was viewed as somewhat radical at the time, although
today it is widely accepted as the way we humans seem to operate.
When our beliefs and behavior don't match up, he asserted, we
experience psychological discomfort or "cognitive dissonance."
This dissonance cannot be tolerated for long, and provides a powerful impetus for change. We can change either our belief or our
behavior, according to Festinger—either one will reduce the dissonance. Aspects of our self-concept, however, are deeply held and
therefore more resistant to change. In such cases, it is easier to
alter our behavior so that it corresponds with our self-concept
than it is to alter our very identity.

By complimenting me on how thorough I was, my dad broad-
ened my self-concept in a positive way. He gave me a label that
helped organize the way I thought about myself and the work I
did. It was easier to mop the entire kitchen and do a good job of it
than it was to give up the thought of myself as thorough. It was
easier to rake up all the leaves in the yard than it was to do the job
halfway and risk tarnishing my reputation.

This strategy works just as well with younger kids. One summer afternoon Jenny and I took our kids to visit her parents. Four-
year-old Ryan was being a little too rambunctious with his little

brother and younger cousin. Knowing that we would be there the entire evening (and that it would be a long night if this continued), I took him aside for a minute. "Ryan, Mom and Dad are going to be upstairs tonight while you and the other kids are in the basement. When you're all playing together, some of the kids will need to be tended, and some of them will be big helpers. What do you think about Emily? [She was his older aunt.] Does she need to be tended?"

"No."

"Right, she's a big helper. What about baby Alex, is he a big helper?"

"No, he needs to be tended."

"Right. What about you?"

Ryan grinned and bounced up and down in his seat. "Big helper!" he said with a tilt of his head.

That was the extent of our conversation. For the rest of the night, the kids played happily downstairs while we adults visited upstairs in peace. A couple of times we went downstairs to compliment them and encourage more of the same, but nothing else they did required our intervention.

Ryan had a strong need to feel that he was getting bigger and more mature. We adults wanted to be able to visit in peace. Looking back, this strategy of "exploiting" worked better than scolding or threatening or constant monitoring.

So go ahead and exploit your child's self-esteem. You'll both be better off. It's the kind of exploitation that should go on in every family.

Give Them More Power

To stay in charge as a parent, give your kids more power? Flies in the face of reason, doesn't it? But it really works.

I remember watching my in-laws struggle to get their twelve-year-old son, Brad, to do his chores. It was more work for them than it was for him. Constant reminders, encouragement, threats, and checkups of his work were a part of their daily routine. The older he got, the more resistant he became. They were pulling their hair out.

They decided they needed to try a different approach. They assigned each of the children two rooms in the house—his or her own and one other. The children were responsible for keeping those rooms clean and in order. The kitchen rotated between kids and parents.

With Brad, this strategy worked better than his parents had hoped or even dreamed. To everyone's surprise, the family room, Brad's domain, quickly became the most immaculate room in the house. Rather than their having to battle with the kids to keep things clean, Brad was the one on guard duty. He reminded others—in his not-so-subtle twelve-year-old way—not to leave things out in his zone: "If you're going to make a mess, do it in your own territory!" He vacuumed three or four times a week. Occasionally he rearranged the furniture. He even started chopping the firewood himself, keeping a store of it stacked neatly by the fireplace, and he stoked the fire on cold evenings.

As a frequent visitor to their home, I'll attest that the family room became the most comfortable room in the house. Brad developed quite the reputation among relatives and family friends. He was embarrassed by all the attention he got for his work. And he loved every minute of it.

A sense of ownership led Brad to take pride in his work. Before, being a take-charge kind of guy had meant proving that he didn't have to do what his parents told him. Now, taking charge meant doing exactly what his parents wanted. Instead of fighting with Mom and Dad, he could channel his energy and sense of power into doing his work and insisting that other family members respect his domain. He still had the energy to put up a fight, and he got pretty animated at times with his brothers and sisters. But now at least he and his parents were on the same side.

One morning I stayed home with Ryan, who was then three years old, and his little brother, Aaron, while Jenny was out running errands. This was a change in their routine; the boys were used to seeing their mom in the morning. Aaron, who was eighteen months old at the time, woke up and was all smiles. He saw Dad and concluded that it was play time. But for Ryan it was a different story. He wasn't happy to see me. He wanted his mom. He cried and kicked and screamed.

There was no consoling Ryan, so, after a couple of minutes of trying, I decided it was time for plan B. *Maybe if I ignore Ryan, he'll get over it,* I thought. I took Aaron downstairs and began getting breakfast for him, talking loudly enough that Ryan could hear me from his room.

"Aaron, I guess we'll get you some juice, and a granola bar . . ."

Ryan called out, "Don't give him a gorilla bar. Aar-Bear won't eat 'em. He hates 'em and he just crumbles 'em everywhere and then you have to clean it up." Ryan marched down the hallway and into the kitchen.

"What shall I feed him, then?"

"He likes toast."

"With jam on it?"

"No, just butter."

Next thing I knew, Ryan was telling me all about their morning schedule and about how Mom started them with breakfast and then it would be time for a bath and I shouldn't let the baby stand up in the bathtub.

What had changed?

Ryan had moved into a position of responsibility, and that had elicited competencies and abilities that hadn't been apparent just moments earlier. Instead of needing to be helped to cope with Mom's absence, he became the guide. This task demanded his sensibilities, which he had developed over time because Mom trusted him and taught him and held him responsible.

We can hand over power to our kids in all sorts of ways, helping them become more responsible:

"I can't do this job by myself, I need some muscle in here."

"Are you big enough to do this job, or shall I have your sister help you?"

"I want you to decide the best way to organize these toys."

"What would you like to do first, take out the garbage or watch the rest of your show?"

Obviously, this strategy will break down at times. ("Mom, I thought you wanted me to help because I am so big and now you tell my four-year-old brother the same thing?") But sometimes it works. And when it does, it not only improves children's behavior at that moment but gives them an added sense of autonomy and self-control that will surely work for their good in the future.

CHANNEL THEIR ATTENTION BACK TO THE CHOICES THEY CAN MAKE

At times it is appropriate to give our kids more power, but if we were to give them all the power they wanted, they might not stop until they ruled the neighborhood. That state of affairs would be bad for our kids and even worse for the rest of the people on the block. So, as parents, we reserve the right to make many choices for our children. Sometimes we do so for their safety; sometimes it's for our sanity. Then again, sometimes we take charge solely for simplicity's sake.

On occasion we may ask our kids what they would like for dinner, for instance, but most of the time they just have to eat what we are fixing. When they disagree with our choice, how do we respond? Let's consider some options:

Child: "I hate chicken!"

Parent: "Why can't you just eat what I fix without complaining for once? I work my tail off around here, and rarely do I get a word of thanks."

A valid point—one that will not, however, register with the child. What might be going on in the child's mind? *It was really a lot of work to create this disgusting mess. What does that have to do with the fact that it nauseates me?*

Let's consider another possible response:

Child: "I hate chicken!"

Parent: "What would you rather have?"

Bad choice. The last thing we want to do is fix the children a special, made-to-order dinner. If we are going to do that, we may as well have them plan out their menus for the next forty years—after all, they will stick around if we give them the kind of service they can't get anywhere else.

On the other hand, if we don't plan on fixing what they want, it's best if they don't dwell on it. So let's try again:

Child: "I hate chicken!"

Parent: "Don't you want big muscles? Chicken has protein, and that's what it takes to make you grow big and strong!"

Great sales pitch. Excellent logic. The problem is, this tactic doesn't even work for adults. ("This low-fat diet is really going to pay off in the long run.") To kids, the distant future is even less compelling. So what is a parent to do? How about channeling the child's attention back to the choices he or she is free to make? Try the following:

Child: "I hate chicken!"

Parent: "Do you want barbecue sauce or honey to dip it in?"

Child: "I hate chicken!"

Parent: "Do you want three or four carrots to go with it?"

Child: "I hate chicken!"

Parent: "Do you want a full glass of milk, or just a half?"

Child: "I hate chicken!"

Parent: "Would you like to eat it with a fork, or shall I get you a toothpick?"

Child: "I hate . . . I want to eat it with a toothpick."

Parent rises to get the box of colorful toothpicks. "Would you like to use a red toothpick or a blue one?"

Child: "Blue."

If the above exchange sounds too good to be true, let me assure you that I've used this strategy many times with my own kids, and with good results. As with any of the other tactics we have explored, it doesn't work all the time. However, when it does work, sometimes it works like a charm.

When our son Aaron was three, he used to fight bedtime. We spent many nights peeling tiny fingers from stair railings and door frames. He would plead and we'd explain: "You can't stay up any later. It'll make you too tired to play tomorrow. Bodies need to rest." None of our explanations had much effect. Even when everyone's energy was finally exhausted and he had given up for the night, we knew he was like a little General MacArthur: "I shall return." The battle may have ended, but the war would continue the following evening.

Then one day we hit upon this idea of directing his attention back to a realm of control that was appropriate for him, back to the range of choices he *could* make on his own. He couldn't determine his own bedtime, but what choices was he still free to make?

Mom: "Aaron, it's bedtime."

Aaron: "No!"

Mom: "Would you like to take your blanket with you or not?"

Aaron: "I'm playing!"

Mom begins leading Aaron down the hallway to his room: "Would you like to have the light on or off?"

Aaron: "I don't want to go to bed! . . . on!"

Mom: "Do you want to take a toy or a book to bed?"

Aaron (after a short pause): "A book." Sniffle.

Mom: "Do you want to read *A Wocket in Your Pocket* or *Curious George*?"

With some physical prompting from Mom, Aaron climbs onto his bed: "*Curious George*. But I want the blue *Curious George* book."

Mom: "Is this the right one?"

Aaron: "Yeah. Mom, did you know the man with the yellow hat had to pick up Curious George in a helicopter when he flew his kite too high?"

Mom: "Show me."

The more we discuss bedtime, the more we discuss the dream graduation trip to Jamaica, the more we discuss the new seven-foot Barbie skyscraper, the more we encourage our kids to focus their attention on options that are not realistic. However, if we keep our wits about us, we can avoid following their lead into thinking about a dilemma as they have defined it. We can remind them that, even when they don't get exactly what they want, there is an entire range of options still available to them. By the way we respond, we can channel their attention back to the vast realm of power that is more appropriately theirs.

Recognize and Get Out of Tailspins

Your child refuses to come home from playing when you call from the front porch. You yell at him, "Get in here right now!" He runs. You chase him. He ducks into your neighbor's garage. You grab his arm to drag him home. He screams. You squeeze his arm harder. He starts to kick. You spank. He bites. You put him in his room. He kicks a hole in the wall. And . . . well, you get the picture.

This is an example of a parenting tailspin. Your child does something that aggravates you and you do something punitive in response. Not to be outdone, your child then ups the ante. Indignant, you raise your voice and threaten harsher punishment. You try to take control, but your efforts just seem to make things worse.

For aviators, a tailspin is dangerous because attempts to solve the problem serve only to exacerbate it. The same thing can be true for parents. When our children defy us, how do we respond? We try to show them who's boss. So whatever the initial reason for the defiance, now they recognize, "This is about who's the boss over me." And who is the boss over them? Ultimately, they are! And because they are, we can never win a battle once our children have defined it in this way.

I've been surprised by the power of the tailspin phenomenon in my own life as a parent. When one of my kids starts into a full-fledged tantrum, sometimes I catch myself making threats and hollering away. I act this way even though it has never worked to calm my children down! Unless the cycle is interrupted, the situation continues to spiral downward in a tailspin. Occasionally the child will "snap out of it" before things deteriorate too far. Usually though, it's up to the parent to stop the cycle.

Once they get started, how can we exit such tailspins? The solution is quite simple, although it's by no means easy to employ. We must refuse to let our kids' behavior drag us into the pattern. At any point in time we have the power to interrupt the downward spiral by changing our own attitude, actions, and words.

Bill O'Hanlon, a family therapist practicing at the Hudson Center in Omaha, Nebraska, tells a story of one mother he worked with. She was having tremendous trouble with a daughter who sometimes got so grouchy she would ruin the day for both of them.

"Funny thing is," the mom said, "I can tell first thing in the morning whether it's going to be a good day or a bad day."

"How's that?" Bill asked.

"When she wakes up with a big smile on her face, it will be a good day. On the bad days, I hear a moan and a whine from her room first thing. Then I grit my teeth and prepare for a battle."

"Well, we can't control her," Bill said, "but let's look at how you're responding to her. What's your reaction when she's cheerful?"

"I walk in her room, sit down on her bed, and kind of play with her: 'There's my little sunshine! Hi sweetie-pie! How's Momma's little girl?' "

"What about when she's cranky?" Bill asked.

"I usually scold her: 'You have no reason to be this way with me, young lady. Straighten up or you're going to lose some privileges.' "

Bill suggested that this mother interrupt her own reaction and try behaving in exactly the same way no matter how her daughter seemed in the morning: "Do your sunshine-sweetie-pie routine no matter what you see or hear when you step into her room."

The mother tried his suggestion and found that, although not every day was perfect, it did seem to help. As Mom continued to hold her ground, eventually good days replaced most of the bad.

We must become more aware of the signs that tell us things are spiraling out of control. The fact that the mother in the above story *knew* her day was ruined if her daughter woke up on the wrong side of the bed was a clue that she was following her daughter's lead into a tailspin. That can be a great clue for us too. When we can predict exactly how things will turn out—and it's not an outcome we prefer—we're probably following our child's lead. But as soon as we recognize that we're stuck in a tailspin, we are no longer truly stuck. We can interrupt the cycle and choose more creative responses.

It's easy to blame our kids for the way we act when we continue the tailspins they initiate. But it takes two to tango; if one bows out, the dance is over. Ultimately, the power remains in our hands.

So, next time your child picks a fight, try sticking with your sunshine-sweetie-pie routine.

Play Pygmalion

There are certain helpful tricks we can play on ourselves as parents. While they may start out as mind games, they end up
influencing more than just our own psyches—they can change our
children's lives. I'll give you the recipe for one of these tricks, but
before I do, let me tell you how I know it really works, so you
don't think this is just snake oil I'm peddling.

In the late 1960s, Harvard psychologist Robert Rosenthal
teamed up with an elementary school principal named Leonore
Jacobson to do some ingenious research. They gave children in
Jacobson's elementary school a bogus test they called the Harvard
Test of Mental Fluctuancy. It was not actually designed to measure
anything, but Rosenthal and Jacobson's story to the teachers was
that it measured the probability that a given child would "bloom"
academically during the coming school year.

The researchers wanted to see what kind of effect teachers'
expectations might have on children's actual performance. They
labeled six children in each classroom "academic bloomers." Of
course, they identified these children not with the phony test but
by using a table of random numbers—essentially drawing their
names from a hat. This way they knew that any later difference in
performance between kids was truly due to the way they were
treated by teachers.

What Rosenthal and Jacobson found was that the teachers'
anticipation of rapid academic development in the chosen children led to actual improvement in those children's scores on

intelligence tests. The scores of children labeled bloomers improved an average of six points more than those of the other students in the school during that same time period. In that study and others by Rosenthal since then, he has discovered that we do treat people differently based on our expectations. Teachers spend more time with students whom they expect to do well, ask them more questions, ask them more difficult questions, and are not as accepting of substandard performance.

Rosenthal called this phenomenon "Pygmalion in the classroom." Pygmalion was the character in Ovid's tale of classic mythology who, dissatisfied with the living women of the time, chiseled a statue of a beautiful woman he named Galatea. He became so infatuated with his work that he pined away for her, wishing that she would come to life. Eventually, Venus took pity on him and brought Galatea to life. The strength of Pygmalion's desire for Galatea had been so compelling that eventually the real world patterned itself after his fantasy.

Rosenthal's research powerfully demonstrated what he called the self-fulfilling prophecy. If we expect something from someone in a relationship, our expectation alone can powerfully influence future reality. And self-fulfilling prophecies do not operate only in the classroom. Subsequent research by Rosenthal and others has verified their power in many other types of relationships.

The way we treat people tends to make our beliefs about them come true. Years and years before Rosenthal's research, Goethe knew this. "If you treat a man as he is, he will stay as he is," he taught, "but if you treat him as if he were what he ought to be, and could be, he will become that bigger and better man."

How can we, as parents, apply these ideas? Perhaps the implications are obvious, but we mustn't take them too far. Remember, researchers found only a difference of six points in the IQs of "academic bloomers"—they didn't necessarily become geniuses. So we shouldn't assume that we can choose what we want our kids to be and then force them into that mold. I've seen too many adults who still have a sour taste in their mouth from their overambitious dads on the sidelines during Little League games. Goethe also warned, "We can't form our children to our own concepts; we must take them and love them as God gives them to us." We cannot raise a child to become a Mozart or a Joe Montana, a Meryl Streep or a Martina Navratilova, just because we have such grandiose visions.

However, we can be on the lookout for seeds of greatness in our children. Every human being has areas in which he or she can excel. What is your child's forté? Identify one or two strengths, and then act with confidence that your child will "bloom." More than likely you'll begin to see what you're looking for, at least in part *because* you looked for it and acted in ways that conveyed your confidence. It's as simple as that.

Use Their Imagination

Having forgotten what it was like to be a kid, I find that it is all too easy to dismiss my children's concerns and downplay their fears. Respecting their perspective might stretch imagination to its limits, but it is worth the effort.

Along these lines, I once heard a father describe how he had finally helped his son overcome his fear of "dark monsters" in his bedroom. At first, he tried to talk his son out of his fear, explaining, "There's no such thing as monsters." His argument was earnest and his logic was sound, but the boy remained unconvinced.

Dad's persistence didn't pay off. So one day, on a whim, he went along with his boy's imagination. "See my new sword?" he asked one evening as he entered his son's bedroom, acting as though he were clasping the hilt of an imaginary saber. "It's a monster-killer." The boy's eyes danced as he considered the implications of his dad's new approach.

"Oh, Dad, that'll do it! Now we'll get 'em for sure," the boy said, bouncing up and down as he sat on the bed.

"You call me if any of them come around, and I'll be here as quickly as I can."

Unaware of what it was in for, a "dark monster" showed up again that night. But instead of a helpless little victim, it had to contend with the boy's father. Dad emerged victorious, of course, but when the battle was over, he warned the boy: "I only wounded him, and then he got away. He may be back, but now you know how to use this thing." He reached down and placed the imaginary sword on the boy's pillow. "I'll leave it here just in case you need it."

Sounds of sword fighting came from the boy's room several times that week. But he never again complained to Dad. Apparently those battles were nothing he couldn't handle on his own, now that he had his own monster-killer.

Sometimes we worry that a child's unrealistic concerns will balloon even further out of proportion if we treat them seriously. We are afraid that children will work themselves into a frenzy unless we take such "trivial" matters lightly. Surprisingly, it is usually the other way around: Once a child has talked something over, it no longer feels so pressing. Just sharing a concern with a parent who is obviously really listening can provide tremendous relief. Of course, showing the child how to use a monster-killer sword doesn't hurt, either.

Hypnotize Them

As a psychologist, I know that what a stage hypnotist does to audience members is not magic. Hypnosis is not voodoo. It's merely a heightened state of suggestibility.

As parents, we can learn a thing or two from hypnotists. We can use some of the tricks of their trade to make our kids more receptive to our guidance and directions. Don't worry, no dangling pocket watches or spiral disks required. Those are not the key ingredients of the hypnotists' approach. Here are their real secrets:

1. Command the attention of your subjects. The first thing hypnotists do is direct the attention of those they are trying to influence: "Look at the light" or "Notice now that your hands feel heavy."

2. Create an emotional climate that encourages cooperation. Stage hypnotists try to create an atmosphere that is comfortable yet exciting. They're hoping to have subjects who are willing and energetic.

3. Continue directing your subjects' attention while you apply subtle guidance. It's a myth that hypnotists overpower their subjects with commands. Instead of being pushy, they use phrases like "you *may* begin to sway back and forth" or "*perhaps* your chair is getting hotter."

Stage hypnotists are not the only ones who use these principles of influence. Consider advertising. The above steps capture the essence of what advertisers try to achieve. They get our attention, create a mood, and plant a suggestion. We see a family having fun together at the park (they have captured our attention and triggered warm feelings). Then we see or hear the name of their product (they've applied subtle guidance). Advertisers have learned that no logical argument can match the power of this kind of hypnotic suggestion.

Let's examine how these principles can be applied by parents. First, consider a typical attempt to influence a child without the use of hypnosis:

"Kevin, it's time to brush your teeth."

"No, I'm playing."

"Kevin, come here. I'm going in to get your toothbrush, and you'd better be in the bathroom by the time I get the toothpaste on it."

Kevin continues playing.

A minute later Dad takes Kevin into the bathroom by the arm.

"Open your mouth."

"No! I don't like it. Yucky." Kevin starts crying.

"I know you don't like it, but you don't want to get cavities, do you? If you don't brush, your teeth will get rotten and fall out."

"No, Dad!"

"I'm sorry, honey, we all have to brush our teeth, whether we like it or not."

Now, here's an example of how hypnosis might (on our lucky days) defuse this kind of struggle:

"Kevin, it's time to brush your teeth."

"No, I'm playing."

"Kevin, do you remember last month when we went fishing?"

Dad is directing Kevin's attention. He wants Kevin to be a willing participant, so he directs him to focus on something besides the brushing of teeth.

Kevin's eyes light up. "Yeah," he says with a smile.

"Did you catch a fish?"

"Yeah."

Kevin is more likely to be friendly and cooperative when he's think-ing about fishing, one of his favorite pastimes. Dad has just succeeded in creating a receptive emotional climate.

"How big was it?"

"Like this!" Kevin gestures with his hands.

"Here we go," Dad says quietly as he lifts Kevin to a standing position. "That *is* big."

Dad's suggestions are both verbal ("here we go") and nonverbal (lifting Kevin to a standing position). This guidance is subtle, and Dad continues to direct Kevin's conscious attention to the memories of an enjoyable fishing trip.

"Whose boat did we go on?" Dad asks as he guides Kevin to the bathroom with a hand on his shoulder.

"Grandpa's."

"Did anyone else catch a fish?"

"Au-sha-wu."

Kevin tries to say "Aunt Sharon," but it's hard to talk with a tooth-brush in your mouth.

This strategy may seem a bit weird at first, but before you knock it, you really ought to try it out. In fact, as you read this, you just may be feeling more and more like giving it a try . . . today. You may . . . be feeling . . . more and more . . . like giving . . . it a try.

Back Up Your Words with Action

When you say, "How many times have I told you?" and the child can't count that high, you are probably talking too much.

"How many times have I asked you to pick up after yourself?" Next time, don't ask. You come into the front room, and there are toys and homework and a Walkman and other stuff all over. Don't even open your mouth. Open a giant trash bag instead. Fill it up with all the stuff that was left out, lock it in your closet, and at the dinner table say: "I was glad to pick up after you all. If ever you can't find anything you left out where it shouldn't be, come see me. I probably picked it up for you. And I'll be happy to . . . sell it back to you."

More action, fewer words. That may sound exhausting at first. *I'll have to intervene constantly,* you may be thinking. But parents who implement this idea find that every time they take action, their words gain more power. Suppose you say once, "Lori, don't sit on your sister." Lori keeps sitting on her sister. Instead of repeating, "Lori, I told you not to sit on your sister," three or four more times, repeat it maybe one more time. If that doesn't do it, then physically separate them—impose a time-out, if that's what you do—and the fun is over. The next time you say, "Lori, don't sit on your sister," or give her some other direction, she'll know that Dad says it once or twice, and then follows through. She has learned: *That was his final warning; I'd better move now if I want to stay here and play.*

If action comes only at the end of a long monologue, kids figure out they are free to ignore the first nine-tenths of the lecture.

Action is not the last resort in child-raising. Frequent action is what we owe our children—and the younger they are, the more active we'll need to be. The best way to teach our children the power of our words is to back those words up with prompt action.

Make Bad Behavior Costly

What teenager doesn't love to do this: keep pushing the limits of patient, long-suffering parents, until POW! "I'm so angry at you, son! I can't stand it anymore! You rgrah rgrah rgrah, rgrah rgrah rgrah, rgrah rgrah rgrah!"

And he sits back and feigns concern. "Gee, Mom, pull yourself together. You're usually so reasonable. Why didn't you say something? I'm perfectly calm about this, and it's abundantly clear to the younger kids here and to our neighbors watching us out their back window that I would respond to calm, rational discussion."

Sometimes as parents we are "fair" and "reasonable" for too long, until finally we've had enough and we explode! That's why I believe in guerrilla parenting. *Guerrilla warfare* is defined as a situation in which the warring parties fail to adhere to the rules of conventional warfare. So *guerrilla parenting* is when parents don't adhere to the rules of conventional parenting.

What are the strategies of guerrilla parenting? What do we do instead of waiting and tolerating and talking "reasonably" until we're blue in the face? The first thing we can try is to make the behavior we want to stamp out more costly for the child than it is for us.

For a long time my mom told me and my brothers to shut the door gently instead of letting it slam when we left the house. For a while she reasoned with us: "It will wake up your little brother. It's hard on the door. Sometimes it stays open and bugs get in the house."

She was very patient. She would reason and reason and reason. "Please don't slam . . . please don't slam . . . please don't slam . . ." Finally she exploded. "Stop it! Stop slamming that door!"

But apparently neither her reasoning nor her exploding made any difference, because she kept doing both, in turn, and that door kept slamming.

Then one day, there was no more reasoning. There were no more explosions. There was just a terse note on the door:

"10 cents per slam."

I still remember, not long after the note was posted, running out the front door to play and hearing the slam behind me. I cringed as the sound echoed in my head. "Augh! . . . No!"

I sneaked back in and walked down the hall to check out the ledger my mom had posted. Sure enough, there was a 10-cent charge underneath my name. Slamming the door had begun to cost me more than it cost my mom. And I was a new man when it came to exiting the house.

Is this kind of guerrilla parenting sneaky? Yes. Manipulative? Maybe. Harmful or wrong? Absolutely not. It is simply a way to conserve our energy for the things that really matter, and therefore be more helpful to our kids.

Keep Expectations Realistic

When our parenting efforts fail, we need to stop and reevaluate. It may be that we need to keep doing what we have already been doing. It may be that we need to do more. It may be that we need to try something new. However, if our children don't respond as we would like, we shouldn't count out the possibility that our sights may just be set too high.

I once worked with Catherine, a severely handicapped preschooler. In an effort to help her develop physical strength, we tried to get her to maintain a sitting position. It was a strain for her, and she occasionally protested with a moan or a cry during the exercise. Frequently she would turn her body to the side and allow herself to collapse gently to the mat on which she was sitting. Those of us who worked with her occasionally referred to this behavior as "oppositional." She wasn't cooperating with our attempts to help, we thought. One day, Catherine's physical therapist came to visit the classroom during our exercise time. As Catherine leaned over and rested on the mat, I made reference to this "resistant" behavior.

"Oh, no," the therapist assured me, "she's not resisting your help. Rolling over like that is merely an indication that she has reached the limits of her physical ability. Her muscles become fatigued and eventually give out on her."

As a parent, I've caught myself occasionally overestimating my kids' ability. When I assume they could do better, and they don't,

I sometimes attribute to them more devious intentions than they are probably capable of.

Barbara and David Bjorklund, authors of *Parents Book of Discipline* (New York: Ballantine, 1990), point out that the misdeeds of children, particularly young ones, quite often result from their increasing curiosity and power to explore their world. Rules are easily forgotten, especially in the temptation of the moment. Children may even simply be checking to see whether yesterday's rules still apply today. The important thing to remember as parents is that such behavior is typically not malicious or even planned.

Our kids may not be conniving. They may not be lazy. As difficult as it sometimes is to believe, they may have no "master plan" that includes our demise. They're just kids, doing exactly the kinds of things kids do. Maybe we need to relax and give them the space to do those things for a while.

PART 4

SURVIVING AN INVASION

WE PARENTS USED TO be a superpower. We used to be respected around the galaxy. Creatures from other planets would talk about us with a sense of awe and respect. They knew that Earthlings were not to be messed with.

But oh, how times have changed! The Russian word for our new interplanetary stance is glasnost: "the new openness." This change has been a good one, for the most part. In some ways, relationships between the planetary species have never been better. Earthlings are viewed as friendlier folks. Jovians have lost much of their fear of us and are more likely to approach us about important interplanetary matters.

As far as I can tell, one of the few problems with this new openness is that Jovians now know we are just human. They are no longer in awe. In fact, they have discovered that we can be downright wimpy. As a result, they have been planning an invasion. And, in case you haven't noticed, they have already begun carrying it out. They would never annihilate us; why should they? After all, dead Earthlings don't make very good servants. That's right: When these aliens land, they don't ask us to take them to our leader. Their objective is much more ambitious; they are interested in becoming our leaders!

Fortunately, their intentions aren't sinister. Even though they try to take over, deep down they don't really want to be in charge. Kids may fight for the job, but they are never comfortable as commanders-in-chief. They feel out of place. They know they need our guidance. We provide structure and firm limits that comfort them immensely. Although they will put up a fight, their battle for dominance is one they are better off losing. They can get everything they need without being the boss. At some point, they may even thank us for staying in charge. But to see that day, we must withstand whatever offensive they organize today. To do that, we need some strategies for staying in charge.

WHO'S IN CHARGE?

Tommy, it's time to eat."

Tommy keeps playing.

"Tommy, it's time to eat! Did you hear me? Dinner is ready, come and get it!"

"I'm not hungry."

The family starts eating without Tommy. A minute later, he comes in.

"Yuck," he announces. "I hate buffalo burgers."

The very term *buffalo burgers* was an invention designed to coax Tommy into eating meat instead of mac and cheese for every meal. They've had pterodactyl wings, alligator tails, you name it.

"How about some potatoes?"

"Yuck, I hate potatoes."

He doesn't. He loves potatoes.

"How about some vegetables?"

"Yuck, I hate carrots! I want some fish sticks."

Dad, who was enjoying his meal until now, gets up to fix the fish sticks.

"No!" Tommy screams. "I want Mom to do it!"

Mom, mumbling something under her breath, gets up to fix the fish sticks.

Little Tommy is not an evil child. He's not even unusual. Given the chance, most kids will take charge of the family.

Little Tommy's parents are not imbeciles. They're not even incompetent. They're like most parents. It's not that they ever made an executive decision to hand over their parental control. It began in subtle ways, giving in here and there to buy a little peace, until one day they found themselves wondering when and how Tommy had taken over.

The good news is, we live in a time of unprecedented respect for children. We recognize their inherent value and goodness. As a society and as families, we're finally putting kids first.

Now for the bad news. We seem to be putting kids first and, in the process, handing over to them control of family life. We're convinced of our children's "inherent worth," all right—so convinced, in fact, that we're afraid we may ruin them by intervening in their lives.

The pendulum has swung too far. We believe in our kids, but we've lost faith in ourselves. And so now, perhaps more than ever, parents are failing to take charge of family life.

Kids are quite satisfied with this arrangement. At least they seem to be, at first. They find this kind of power intoxicating. Not knowing quite what to do with themselves, they try just about everything. But life without boundaries can be disconcerting. When children explore, hoping to find the limits, they get scared when they discover there are none.

How did family life get to this point? How did we lose faith in ourselves, in our kids' need for strong parents? I had an experience lately that provided me with at least one clue. Jenny and I attended a small get-together of acquaintances. There were couples of all ages in the room. It so happened that in the middle of our chat, the diaper of a one-year-old who was playing on the floor started to stink up the place. The baby's mother and father, a twenty-something couple, looked at each other. The husband gave a subtle nod of his head, as if to say, "I'll get this one." He gathered the gear he would need and headed toward the bathroom. As he was leaving, I looked across the room at a gentleman in his fifties.

Watching the young father, he shifted in his seat. He rubbed his face with his hand vigorously, smiling nervously. I wondered if perhaps his masculinity was being threatened vicariously.

This older man's wife also saw the young man exit with the baby and a diaper in hand. Her mouth dropped open, and she tilted her head and exclaimed, "How *nice* of him!"

Struck by their reaction, I looked around the room. What I saw was a clear split, right down generational lines. One of the other older men in the room watched in awe and respect, as though a good buddy had just volunteered for battle duty. On the other hand, the event had gone mostly unnoticed by the younger couples. Apparently the only thing that caught their attention was the comment, "How nice of him!" At this, the wife of the diaper-changer smiled. One of the younger men looked around quizzically, as if to ask, "Did I miss something?"

The role of fathers is changing. We have become much more proficient at kissing owies, wiping bottoms, fixing bottles, cooking dinners, and changing diapers.

Don't buy the typical male explanation of this transition. It's not that we're more enlightened today. That's not it at all. It's that mothers decided they'd had enough. They were tired of doing all the day-to-day work of nurturing. At some enormous, secret convention, they all voted to bring fathers into the thick of it. There were those rare males who were nurturers even before, but since this secret gathering, men have been involved whether they liked it or not.

Hearty gender that we are, we males have managed to adapt. Perhaps a genetic mutation has occurred. Those without this "nurturing" gene are dying off. Those with the gene are replacing the "macho manly man" as the new breed of dominant (if you can still call him that) male.

Many children now have two parents who are very good at

what was formerly traditionally considered "mothering." This kinder, gentler breed of fathers has, for the most part, been good for kids. Most still prefer their moms, but now their dads can provide many of the same things, in a pinch.

We dads like it too. We are bonding, becoming more connected with our kids. Having tasted the good life—the joy of nurturing—you can bet we will not be fighting for a return to the old way anytime soon.

Our society as a whole is benefiting as well. A dad who is connected is less likely to go deadbeat. He's protective of his kids and has empathy and compassion for them. He has more of a feel for how much they would suffer if he were not there. This change is creating more cohesive family units.

Some kids thrive within this new system. All they need is love and encouragement. Their souls respond, and they soar to reach their potential. I've been privileged to know a couple of such kids myself, though unfortunately not as children of my own.

Fact is, this new wave of fathering is not without its pitfalls. The dynamics of family life have shifted. When fathers kept a bit of emotional distance from their kids, setting limits and saying no was a lot easier. As their emotional intimacy with their kids deepens, dads are not as able to be the "bad guy." They are learning what moms have always known: It's hard to be stern with those you're used to supporting. "You just wait 'til your father gets home" really means, "I don't have the heart to discipline you like I know you need it."

Many have assumed that these old functions of fatherhood firmness could simply be done away with, and that kids would develop just fine. Now we're discovering that we abandon them to our own peril, and to the peril of our children. Our entire society is paying the price. Most kids still do need more than just "mothering." They need a firm hand of guidance, a voice that is stern at times, a refusal to be swayed by pleading, crying, or intimidation.

This is no longer a job for dads alone. Just as parents now share the burden of nurturing, for the sake of the kids they also need to take charge together.

Earthlings, Unite!

Helping kids grow up to be responsible adults is a daunting task. Some people say it takes a village to raise a child. I don't think that's overstating it. After all, doesn't it take an entire moving crew just to get a sixteen-year-old out of bed in the morning?

You will increase your effectiveness as a parent by forming a network of people who back you up and will shore up your authority. The following suggestions may help you develop and maintain this kind of powerful support system.

1. *Cooperate with your spouse.* Confer regularly so that your actions make sense to each other. Consult with your spouse about sticky issues in advance—and in private when possible—so that the two of you can present a united front when you face the kids.

Support your spouse's efforts at discipline, and solicit his or her support in yours. Sometimes kids come to one parent pleading the details of their case against the other. Resist the temptation to be the "good guy" with your kids. Kids are better off learning that if they have received an answer from one of you, the other will uphold that decision. When they know that rules are uniform and come from both Mom and Dad, they're less likely to single out one parent for more pressure. Even when a compromise does seem appropriate, consult each other first, and then inform the child of your decision as a team.

If you disagree about how to handle a situation, find a way to work it out that bypasses regular arguments and conflict. Psychologist Ron Taffel suggests parents might divide the various responsibilities between them. Mom's in charge of dinner; Dad does the bedtime routine. You may even trade off on a regular basis (Dad does dinner on Tuesdays, Thursdays, and Saturdays). Consistency may be ideal, but for centuries kids have somehow managed to cope with two parents' different personalities.

2. *Stay close to extended family.* If you live far away, stay in touch by writing regularly and planning occasional vacations. For some reason, advice from Grandpa or a favorite aunt carries more weight than hearing "the same old thing again" from Mom and Dad. More distant relatives frequently have more influence with a wayward child than parents can. If you've worked to maintain those extended-family relationships, they'll be there as a safety net when you and your kids need it.

I've seen older kids move in with extended family members or close family friends for a time and fly much straighter than when they were with their parents. Occasionally this kind of space can help everyone in the family regain their perspective.

3. *View your child's teachers as partners.* This means supporting them in the demands they make on your child. Meet with them— or at least touch base—regularly. You will help your child succeed in school by backing up his or her teacher.

Also, share with teachers your concerns. They can help address problems during the time they're in charge of your children. They can act as additional sets of eyes and ears to monitor your children's progress. Perhaps most of all, a teacher is another adult who cares deeply about the welfare of your son or daughter.

I'm surprised by the way some parents of troubled kids handle their relationship with that child's teachers. I once worked with a mother and father who were very concerned about their son Scott's deteriorating behavior, including experimentation with drugs and vandalism around the neighborhood. But when we talked about school, they were both protective of Scott and complained about how harsh the school had been in handling problems. It was as though school was the one aspect of Scott's life in which he and his parents were united against a common foe, instead of battling with each other. Even more surprising to me was the fact that they had never been down to the school to talk with his teachers, in spite of the teachers' invitations to meet. Communication had consisted primarily of voice mail, answering machines, and messages passed along by the school secretary.

I had a hunch that by listening only to Scott's side of the story instead of talking with teachers directly, his parents had allowed him to "divide and conquer." I encouraged them to call a conference at the school where we could all meet together—Scott, his parents, his teachers, and I. Mom and Dad were both surprised (although I was not) when both of his teachers (he was in a special class for kids with behavior problems) stayed an hour later than usual to be there at the only time Dad could make the meeting. Mom and Dad were both surprised (although I was not) that the teachers appeared to be rational, caring, and gentle human beings. The parents were also relieved that the demands the teachers were making on Scott were legitimate and reasonable. Scott looked on sheepishly as parents and teachers talked back and forth and got the facts straight. The substance and mood of the session was captured in a dramatic moment toward the end of our meeting. Looking slightly confused, one of the teachers inquired, "So Scott has never been abused at home?" Apparently, Scott had been playing both sides.

Parents need not adopt a detective mentality when communicating with teachers. If you stay in touch over time, the kind of session that Scott's parents had will probably never be needed. In some cases a teacher may truly be unreasonable; by staying in touch you can assess the accuracy of your kid's complaints for yourself. But don't let your child's description scare you off.

Sometimes kids are simply looking for a way to dodge responsibility for their own actions.

When talking with your children, look for excuses to praise and support, rather than question and demean, their teachers and other school officials. Your kids will learn from your example.

4. *Band with other parents who have a similar commitment to their kids.* Get to know other parents in your neighborhood. Get involved in your school's Parent-Teacher Association. Volunteer to help with your church's youth organization. Join a support group for parents. You'll feel stronger just knowing your peers share your concerns and struggles. Their moral support may be just what you need to take on the difficult tasks that send many parents running.

5. *Encourage your child's involvement with peers who share your values.* On July 29, 1994, 500,000 cards pledging chastity until marriage were displayed on the mall in Washington, D. C. The event was a conference of Baptist teenagers. In addition to other activities, they were participating in the "True Love Waits" campaign, a movement that had gotten started some months earlier in a small Baptist church in Nashville, Tennessee. These kids were doing the right thing. And their parents had helped them find a place where they were being praised—instead of teased—for doing it.

Knowing that so many others are making the same commitment can give kids the courage to stand up for their beliefs. University of Tennessee student Susan Fitzgerald said her resolve was strengthened once she got involved in the "True Love Waits" program. "Most all my friends are real supportive, even if they've already had sex," she said. "I even hear some people tell me, 'I wish I would have waited' " (NBC Television, *Today*, September 29, 1993).

6. *Encourage your kids to work part-time.* Kids can invest their creative energy in mischief or in making a productive contribution.

Interacting with employers and customers, they'll realize that Mom and Dad are not the only ones who demand that they do things well. Even younger kids can learn responsibility by baby-sitting, delivering newspapers, or doing yard work for neighbors. Somehow, it's no longer nagging when it's a neighbor who points out the spot they missed with the lawn mower. If we are careful not to let outside work interfere too much with the time we spend together as a family, it can be a great experience for kids.

7. *Seek out other authority figures who share your values and concern for your child.* The Big Brother and Big Sister organizations can help provide the kind of mature and influential role models kids need. Organizations like the YMCA and YWCA are filled with caring adults who are investing time and effort that can benefit your child. Boy Scouts, Girl Scouts, and youth sports programs provide opportunities for children to learn valuable skills as they receive the guidance and support of strong adults. Teachers in school or at church are often important models and mentors besides being instructors.

I recently heard from an appreciative mother in our neighborhood about a visit from three friendly and caring church leaders. During their brief chat with her family, these leaders complimented the kids on their respect for their mother and then managed to extract from them a promise that, beginning the very next day, they would wake up on time, complete their morning chores, and gather for family scripture study and prayer. "These were habits I had been working to establish for a long time with little success," she confided, "so I was blown away the next morning when my kids did exactly as they had committed."

8. *Talk about authority figures in a respectful manner.* I once had a co-worker who complained regularly about his children's lack of respect for his authority. When I also heard him complaining about how highway patrol officers were "out to get us," how the

pastor of his church was a hypocrite, and how Washington, D. C., was full of criminals, I knew where his kids had learned their lack of respect.

Actually, typical police officers are interested in preserving peace and protecting the community. We should teach our children to honor them and support them in their work. We erode that respect when we slam on our brakes and curse every time we see one on the highway.

We can help our kids learn about the immense contribution that is made by the good men and women who invest their time in public service. To do so, we ourselves must look beyond the tabloid headlines and the TV coverage of scandals. When we are involved in our communities, we learn firsthand about all the work that goes on behind the scenes. Then we are in a better position to cultivate our children's understanding of and respect for their leaders.

9. *Find a supportive counselor or therapist.* By no means would I recommend psychotherapy for everyone. But if you're going to get counseling for your child or for your family as a whole, get it from a professional who views the parents as the ones who are and should be in charge. As a psychologist, I'm amazed at how many fellow professionals seem to view kids and parents as equals in every way. They look to the kids as much as they look to the parents when they ask how things ought to be in the home. I'm all for giving kids their domain of authority, but lines should be drawn quite clearly. As family psychologist John Rosemond puts it, families constitute dictatorships, not democracies.

Parents are adults; kids are not. Treating kids as though they are as knowledgeable as their parents only feeds a delusion that some kids (especially teenagers) are more than eager to believe.

In this regard, use your own feelings as a guide. You should generally go away from meetings with a family counselor feeling more competent and powerful as a parent, not feeling discouraged, incompetent, or dependent on your therapist. You and your family will benefit from having a counselor who knows that your kids are kids and that they need your guidance. If your counselor would have you question your own wisdom more than your child's misbehavior, get a new one!

I've also been troubled as I've talked with therapists who seem to feel that their only responsibility is to provide a warm and nurturing environment to kids whose parents aren't quite as caring as they are. Such counselors may empathize so much with their young clients that they only widen the gulf between children and their parents. It's easy to be completely accepting, sympathetic, and supportive when you only have to work with a kid one hour a week. Parents, on the other hand, have to live with that kid full-time. They have to make demands, set limits, and generally be the "bad guy" at times. As a parent, you're much better off taking your children to a professional who will support you in these unpleasant tasks and likewise has the courage to stand up to your kid himself or herself when it's called for.

Communicate regularly with your child's therapist. Some of what goes on in therapy may best be left between your child and his or her counselor. But there's no good reason why two or three adults who are all working for the welfare of a child should not swap impressions and feedback on a regular basis. I learned the importance of this the hard way. Occasionally teenagers attending a drug and alcohol group I helped run would tell the group that their parents refused to come to the family night group sessions. Later we would learn that their parents had never heard about the meetings. I once made the mistake of not contacting, until several weeks into his treatment, the parents of Ben, a sixteen-year-old who was admitted to the inpatient program. During our group sessions, he painted his parents as heavy drug users themselves who had never minded his own use of drugs. I'll never forget my first meeting with Ben's mother. She was horrified by his drug use, worried about his future, and eager to do whatever she could to help in his rehabilitation. The moral for parents is: Always seek your child's input, but don't let it stop you from checking things out for yourself.

10. *Remember, teamwork goes both ways.* Not only do we as families need strong communities, our communities need us! Building strong homes is not enough to stem the tide of moral problems in our society. For our children's sake, we as parents must become involved in building our communities and making them more family-friendly.

Volunteer to baby-sit for friends and neighbors. Become an advocate for social issues that concern children and parents. Attend church and volunteer to teach children's or youth classes. Get involved as a volunteer in community programs designed to support parents. By helping build our communities, we make the tough work of every parent a little bit easier.

We are the only parents our children have. Developing a strong support system will not relieve us of that responsibility. Nor does our help and support relieve other parents of their duties. But teaming up surely can make all of our jobs a lot easier—and increase our chances for success.

Recognize the Virtues of Challenging Children

Annie Sullivan had her hands full with Helen Keller. When the new teacher first arrived at Ivy Green, the Keller family's home in Tuscumbia, Alabama, she found her pupil to be what she was later to describe as a "little savage" (Joseph P. Lash, *Helen and Teacher: The Story of Helen Keller and Anne Sullivan Macy* [New York: AFB Press, 1996], p. 54). Now we look back at what Annie did as heroic, and it certainly was. However, she may not have been so enthusiastic when she met with frustration in her early work with Helen. A showdown of sorts occurred just a short time into their work together:

"I had a battle royale with Helen this morning. Her table manners are appalling. She puts her hands in our plates and helps herself, and when the dishes are passed she grabs them and takes out whatever she wants. This morning I would not let her put her hand in my plate. She persisted and a contest of wills followed. Helen was lying on the floor, kicking and screaming and trying to pull my chair from under me. She pinched me, and I slapped her every time she did it. I gave her a spoon, and held the spoon in her hand, compelling her to take up the food with it and put it in her mouth. In a few minutes, she yielded, and finished her breakfast peaceably. It was another hour before I succeeded in getting her napkin folded" ("An Optimist In Spite of All: Helen Keller's Life Story," audiocassette written and produced by David Freudberg [Cambridge, Mass.: SounDocumentaries, n.d.], side A).

Helen's strength of spirit and vigor were forces to be reckoned with. But in Annie's view, they were not impediments to Helen's growth and education. In fact, later Annie would express strong opinion to the contrary:

"I have always thought I was fortunate in having a wild, wilful and destructive child for a pupil because she was more interesting than a mild, orderly child would have been. Energy is one of nature's choicest gifts to the child. There is always a battle between the vigorous, wilful child and the grown-up who demands submission from him, and many of these splendidly equipped children are destroyed in the process of educating them. They turn to wickedness because of the unnatural restraints and repressions they suffer" (*Helen and Teacher,* p. 348).

That's a refreshing view—particularly when our society so often values conformity over vitality in children.

I am not suggesting that we should do as I saw a parent do recently. His son had dented the neighbor's car with a croquet mallet. This father chalked the incident up to "what an energetic kid he is" and dismissed the matter without a disciplinary consequence of any sort. Remember, Annie Sullivan celebrated Helen Keller's intensity, but she was also active in channeling that energy.

A couple of years ago, in a workshop where parents were bemoaning the challenges of raising strong-willed kids, on a whim I asked, "Looking back at your own childhoods, how many of you can see exactly where your child gets his or her spirited nature?" Most of them—some quite sheepishly—raised their hands. "And look how *you've* turned out," I said, realizing that this thought would be more reassuring to some of the parents than to others.

What was most enlightening to me was to discuss with these parents how their energy and independence were serving them quite well, for the most part, in adult life. One had built his own business as a subcontractor doing stucco work because he couldn't stand to punch a time clock or be at an employer's beck and call.

Another had become a mover and a shaker at the state capitol because, as he put it, "I'm never willing to tolerate the status quo simply because someone in authority tells me 'that's the way it is.'"

In her book *Dreamers, Discoverers and Dynamos* (New York Ballantine, 1999), Lucy Jo Palladino takes a fascinating look at the lives of some of history's more spirited contributors. She shows how Thomas Edison, Anne Morrow Lindbergh, Jesse Owens, Henry Ford, and Emily Dickinson all shared traits that often get kids labeled as "trouble-makers." They were bold, passionate, even headstrong. They were courageous and sometimes outrageous in their willingness to experiment and test the limits. In the end, we remember them for their ingenuity, not their rambunctious nature.

Of course, life is no cakewalk for dreamers, discoverers, and dynamos. The parents who were discussing their own histories at my workshop attributed a share of their challenges to this aspect of their personalities as well. Some confessed a quick temper, a tendency to argue even trivial matters, and a moodiness that can be hard to live with. However, even though their spirited nature at times still landed them in hot water, for the most part they considered this quality a virtue.

Just as our challenging children struggle now, they may have some difficulties when they grow up. That makes it even more critical that they learn to recognize the ways in which their intensity makes their lives better. Thus their view of themselves will be balanced, and their pride and confidence will help inoculate them against the self-doubt and discouragement that might otherwise overwhelm them.

Sometimes Drastic Measures Are Called For

Psychotherapist Craig Berthold sometimes passes along the following story to parents who are having difficulty staying in charge of family life:

There once was a farmer whose cattle kept escaping. They would break down the fence and run loose, sometimes taking hours to round up again. Tired of rounding up cattle and repairing fences, at the advice of a friend the farmer finally put up an electric fence. Caring for his cattle as he did, he decided not to run the full voltage through the wires. They would respond to the discomfort of a mild shock, he reasoned. To the farmer's amazement, his cows kept trying to get through the fence, leaning against it until it threatened to break, in spite of the shock they received. So he turned up the voltage. Once again, the cows were not deterred from testing the fence. Consulting again with his friend, he was advised, "Turn up the voltage to a level that would kill a man, a level that will drop one of your full-grown cows to its knees." The full intensity, it turned out, did the trick. Once they had experienced that strength of shock, the cattle stayed away from the fence.

Even though we always hope our kids will respond to kind and gentle persuasion, sometimes we have to get tough. Gregory Bodenhamer worked as a probation officer in the Orange County, California, youth correction system for years, and has since spent his time teaching parents how to get tough when they need to. In his book *Back In Control* (New York: Simon and Schuster, 1992), he describes some pretty outrageous behavior by kids and the drastic steps some parents had to take to regain their authority. One mother forbade her son to hang out with friends who used drugs. He blatantly defied her appeal, returning to the company of his friends almost immediately. Rather than wringing her hands or cursing his disobedience, she drove to where her son was and ordered him into her car. He refused, adding insult to injury by deriding her with foul language. Refusing to engage in a verbal exchange, this courageous mother got out of her car, kneed her son in the groin, and then, as he doubled over, guided his body into the backseat of her car. This dramatic moment ended up being a turning point in his behavior and in their relationship. By refusing to give up, she had shown her son the depth of her love for him. It's more pleasant when love demands cuddling and sweet words, but at that moment a knee in the groin was the most caring thing she could have done (see pp. 36–37).

I will never forget a story I heard about the master psychotherapist Milton Erikson advising a woman with an out-of-control child to "sit on him for a while the next time he acts out." The woman did, and the child finally sat up and took notice (after his mother had removed her body from on top of him, of course).

I know that some might see the parents' behavior in the examples above as abusive. Actually, I think that getting tough (when truly necessary) helps to prevent abuse more often than not. You see, an interesting thing happens when parents draw the line and stand firm even when kids punish them for it and make the whole thing more of a hassle than it seems parenthood ought to be. Their kids do finally perk up and take notice. Just like the cows who learn to avoid the electric fence, they begin to respect limits instead of constantly testing them.

Here's the key motivation to stand firm: Sending strong messages, when necessary, will eliminate many of the little daily battles that are rampant when kids don't respect limits. Thus, parents will not experience the chronic frustration that accompanies a relentless violation of rules and limits. Getting tough when appropriate may actually decrease the risk of child abuse because parents who are not constantly having their patience tested tend to remain calmer and more respectful of their children.

I once worked with B. J., a ten-year-old who was removed from his parents' custody because they "couldn't control him." When I interviewed B. J. for the first time, he said, "I know I'm bad." When I asked what he meant by that, he said that he never obeyed his parents, he made a mess of the house and refused to clean it up, and he fought constantly with his older brother and sisters.

I asked him what his father would do when B. J. fought with his siblings. "He gets so mad he has to leave," was the answer. I asked what his mom did when he refused to do a chore, like cleaning up his room. "She tries to get me to do it, but when I won't, she cries." In my discussion with B. J., I discovered that these responses—leaving by his father and crying by his mother— were pretty typical of the way they handled problems in the family. As a result, B. J. felt guilty and thought of himself as bad, *but that didn't change his behavior!* It was just too easy to continue misbehaving because no one really forced the issue with him. How much better off B. J. would have been if his parents would have gotten tough and held their ground early on in the process!

When I talked to B. J.'s parents, they said that they had tried and tried to get him to mind, but had finally concluded that it wasn't worth the effort. Since they knew he wouldn't do what they demanded, they stopped requiring it rather than continuing to feel powerless and foolish.

As it turned out, their family was struggling with much more than just B. J.'s behavior. His mother was quite depressed, and there were marital problems that required attention as well. As the parents tried to get their own lives in order and prepared to have B. J. return home, however, I knew that the issue of managing his refusal to cooperate had not gone away. I assured them that they had not been too demanding before, and encouraged them to expect more of B. J. I recommended that when B. J. returned home, they inform him that the rules in their home were the same as before. Furthermore, I recommended that they choose a dramatic and symbolic way to demonstrate to B. J. that they were the parents and he was the child. They decided to take away his radio, his Nintendo, all but two sets of clothing, and all of his Legos, model cars, and other toys and personal belongings in his room. He was informed that from now on, having all of these things was a privilege provided by his parents and he would have to earn that privilege by doing his part—cooperating with them.

Once he returned home, B. J. was an angel. He got all of his stuff back within a few days. That didn't surprise me: Kids often go through this kind of "honeymoon period," particularly when they're afraid they might be rejected if they step out of line. I think B. J. was scared he'd be sent away again if he displeased his parents. On the one hand, it was great that his behavior had improved, but I also knew that fear of exile was not the most healthy motivator. The family had to strike a happy medium somewhere between B. J.'s doing whatever he wanted, as he had before, and walking on eggshells, as he was doing now.

The first true test finally came three and a half weeks after he had returned home. B. J. was informed that he could not go to an air show with his friend's family because he had not done the yard work he had agreed to do before going. He ranted and raved and then retreated to his room, slamming the door behind him. He threw his belongings around the room for a while, breaking the handle off his radio, smashing a plaster eagle statuette, and putting two holes in the walls in the process. The next day, while B. J. was at school, his mother stripped his room of most of his belongings again. That afternoon his dad explained what B. J. would have to do to patch and repaint the walls, and offered to help if B. J. would keep the family car clean for two weeks in return. It took a week or so, but B. J. repaired the damage to his room and earned back his belongings.

When they told me how things had gone, I was now more confident that B. J.'s parents could stand up to anything he could throw at them (both literally and figuratively!). And I knew that B. J. must be gaining respect for their strength. He couldn't walk all over them, and he didn't have to worry about being sent away because of their not being able to handle him. How much better his life was going to be, now that he could trust the limits they set!

Some parents hesitate to take drastic measures because they recognize, quite accurately, that they won't be able to follow through in such a dramatic way each time their child misbehaves. "It would consume too much time and energy—it's not realistic," they argue. But the cows didn't require a high-voltage shock every day to remind them to stay in the field. Once they learned their lesson and understood their limits, they could forget about the fence and get on with the business of eating grass. Similarly, B. J.'s mother could have worked full-time stripping and redecorating B. J.'s room if he had continued to misbehave as much as he had before. But once B. J. knew she was serious, his behavior improved, and she didn't have to.

Using drastic measures on occasion can provide a critical learning experience. Such learning experiences are memorable precisely because they stand out as unusual—even rare—events. For this reason, parents need to become well-versed at using other strategies for staying in charge so that they're not resorting to a howitzer when a flyswatter would do. If you never need drastic measures in your family, consider yourself fortunate. However, if you've tried other strategies and they're just not working, consider designing and implementing a dramatic intervention. You may discover that it's worth the effort.

Don't Overreact to Rebellious Behavior

It's somewhat disheartening to be called a butt-head by your five-year-old. Particularly in front of several neighbors. Particularly when their kids are (at least for the moment) quite well behaved. Particularly when these neighbors know you're a child psychologist who goes to work every day to help other parents manage their children.

It's somewhat disheartening, but not completely discouraging—not when you understand why kids rebel. Kids have many reasons for defying your authority, and watching your face turn blue is not at the top of their list. They do it primarily as an exercise in power. It all starts at about age two, when they discover their bodies are their own. Psychologist Anthony Wolf describes the way this discovery works:

"At some point, most toddlers try the following experiment. Their parent says 'Come here' (or some similar command) and they say 'No.' They then watch to see whose orders their bodies will obey, and they discover that their bodies obey them, not their parents. Usually, children find this discovery quite exciting, and they will repeat this—to them—delightful game. Their parents may find it somewhat less delightful" (*It's Not Fair, Jeremy Spencer's Parents Let Him Stay Up All Night!* [New York: Farrar, Straus and Giroux, 1995], p. 44).

The neighbor kid from whom my child learned the word *butt-head* is not to blame. If my son hadn't learned that word, he would have simply chosen some other way to show me he has a mind of his own. And if that didn't infuriate me, he might experiment until he found something that did. One mother lamented, "Nothing else bothers me quite like Shala telling me she wishes she were dead." Interestingly, that's exactly what little Shala said every time she was angry at Mom. None of my children have yet said they wished they were dead. If they did, I would ignore it and continue on with whatever I was doing. But they don't have to say that when they're angry—I have plenty of other buttons they can push. And they have their ways of finding them.

Kids must do the difficult work of defining who they are. Where does their power end and someone else's (usually Mom's or Dad's) power begin? Sometimes they demonstrate their individuality by demonstrating to themselves and the rest of the world that they're not just a puppet of their parents.

This process may begin at age two, but it won't be over for a long time. All the way through young adulthood, this magical evolution from "part of the family" to "individual" unfolds. Kids don't struggle to develop their identities within a vacuum; a part of "who am I?" becomes "how am I different from others?" Those "others" with whom the child spends most of his or her time tend to be family members.

For firstborn children, this is not always a struggle. After all, just being a kid makes a first child different from his or her parents. For second- and later-born children, however, it can be more complicated. The canvas already has paint on it. Just being themselves may or may not give them a unique identity. Later-born children often declare their independence more vehemently. These dynamics may make them more difficult to manage. Interestingly, research has also shown that a much higher percentage of later-born children become inventors and creators. Firstborns are usually high achievers in more traditional ways; for example, almost all astronauts are firstborns, or at least the oldest son. Later children tend to blaze their own trails rather than follow the more traditional routes to achievement. There is a norm to go against, there are more expectations to violate, and they have more opportunity to do things in unique and creative ways.

I've always liked watching the family dynamics that are played out in the TV series *Family Ties*. Mom and Dad are open-minded, liberal thinkers who would probably respect any lifestyle choice their kids made. After all, they were part of the generation that rebelled against authoritarian oppression in the sixties. How could any child be "different" within this system, in which tolerance and diversity are the dominant values? Ironically, their son, played by Michael J. Fox, finds a way. He joins the Young Republicans. He gets his hair cut short and dresses conservatively—always in a jacket and tie. He carries a briefcase. Predictably, even for his easygoing parents, tolerance has its limits, and he stretches them to the breaking point.

When you see the signs that your child is struggling to differentiate, remember that it is a normal part of growing up. Of course, there may be kids who grow up to be adults without any testing of their parents' values and beliefs. But those aren't the kids whose behavior prompts their parents to pick up a book like this one, now, are they?

Recruit Your Children As Allies

Sometimes it's tempting to play peace officer, judge, and jury in our children's disputes. But when we're trying to solve problems and decrease conflict, it's often wise to recruit the help of the kids themselves.

One single mother had tried for months to get her twelve-year-old daughter and fourteen-year-old son to stop fighting. She was a bright and creative woman—she managed a law office, held a leadership position with the local school board, and was sought out by friends and family for help in decorating their homes. In her business and community, she had the reputation of being efficient and able to solve any problem she tackled. Why did all her attempts to help her kids get along fall flat?

As a last resort, she asked her kids for their ideas. Initially, they responded with sarcasm. "I could move out on my own," her son, Joshua, responded. Celeste, his sister, liked that idea, but Mom had to veto it. Celeste suggested, "I could get my own phone line." Another quick veto. Although it took a while, Mom persisted. Eventually they came up with a list of several suggestions upon which they all agreed:

1. When Celeste's friends are over, Joshua must stay out of the room they're in.

2. Celeste will limit her time in the bathroom to twenty minutes on weekday mornings. She will set a timer and leave it outside the door so Josh will know how long he has to wait.

3. Celeste and Joshua will each give Mom $10 every Sunday.

Whenever one of them insults the other (Mom has to agree it's a put-down), Mom will take one dollar of that person's money and put it in the account of the other. On Saturday afternoon, the one with more than $10 of credit can collect from Mom.

Number three was a real shock to Mom. It's funny how kids can be more severe when determining their own punishment than parents would ever think of being.

These suggestions were by no means any better than what Mom had tried before. In fact, with the exception of number three, they were all slightly altered versions of rules Mom had been trying to enforce all along. But she was willing to give their rules a shot. "Let's see if your suggestions work any better than mine did," she said as they finished the list.

To her surprise, things got better immediately. Celeste collected a total of seven dollars from Joshua over the following two weeks, but there was much less fighting, and most of the time they were actually decent toward one another. Why? What made the difference? Perhaps as ownership of the solution shifted from Mom to Joshua and Celeste, ownership of the problem followed. The kids were more invested in making their own ideas work. If Mom's suggestions failed, what was that to them? In fact, it seemed that they enjoyed batting her suggestions down. However, now their own creativity and intelligence were being put to the test. As a result, they put more effort into reaching what had initially been only Mom's goal.

Even younger children have some good ideas. Have a family meeting and give them a chance. What they come up with may sound silly, but perhaps no more ridiculous than your rules sound to them. Some of their solutions are quite creative. Others are elegantly simple. Of course, a few are laughable, but don't be too quick to write them off.

Clinical psychologist Ron Taffel points out that it can be

amazing how well kids' suggestions sometimes work. He tells the story of a mother who had had no luck solving the problem of getting her son out of bed in the mornings. When she bought him an alarm that was as loud as a foghorn, he turned it off, rolled over, and went back to sleep. If she came into his room and jostled his body a bit, he just moaned. When she got more vigorous and insistent, he yelled at her. Their morning routine made her miserable. By the time she got to work (which was usually about forty-five minutes later than her boss expected), she was exhausted.

When Dr. Taffel solicited suggestions from the son, he said he knew what might work better. "If she sent the dog in to wake me up instead of coming in to do it herself, that wouldn't bother me so much." She started sending the dog in, and the boy started getting up on time in the morning. His idea worked the first time, it worked well, and it has worked ever since!

Kids make pretty potent allies. It's smart for us as parents to do what we can to keep them on our side.

Know When to Get Out of Their Way

Lead, follow, or get out of the way." That is the advice of an old army slogan. But as a pointer to parents, I'd change it a bit: "Lead, sometimes, *by* getting out of the way."

What's our highest priority: gaining power over our kids or empowering our kids? Our goal is not to be in charge of their lives forever. We hope that over time they'll develop the ability to control themselves. We may start out as our kids' bosses, but eventually our role becomes that of outside consultants.

We can't hand over the reins all at once when our kids reach eighteen and are ready to move out of the house. The bestowal of power must be a gradual process. There are no concrete rules for how quickly we should progress in granting them increased independence. As a general guide, however, I like the sentiment expressed in this old Indian saying: "If you make a decision for a child that a child could have safely made for himself or herself, you have just made the child weak."

Most important in our kids' lives is what they do on their own, not what we do for them. (They are keenly aware of this fact, even when we fail to recognize it as parents.) They sense it when the question of who's in charge of their lives becomes all important. Once it seems to them that we care more about being in charge of what they do than we care about them, there's going to be trouble. Then, being in charge becomes their highest priority as well.

I've seen kids sacrifice some pretty important things in their effort to win the battle of control. They reject the values of their parents and society, playing Russian roulette with their health and future by delving into drugs, alcohol, illegal behavior, rebellion at school, and sexual activity.

I once worked with a father who was very worried about his son, Kevin. He didn't want Kevin to play football, and Kevin was rebelling. "Sure, football is popular," I recall the dad saying, "but the pressure to play football is just like the pressure to take drugs or have sex. I think we should all spend our time doing more important things, and I'm just encouraging Kevin to do that." I tried to help this concerned dad see that his attempts to push Kevin were actually working against his intended goal.

When we're uptight and controlling with our kids, they flee from us. Tragically, the choice between their own needs and our demands is not one they want to make, and it's not a choice they should have to make. Unfortunately, Kevin's dad kept at it, refusing to give up the fight and give his son a little more space and a little more power. Kevin dropped out of high school during his junior year and started smoking and drinking, much to his father's dismay. He also moved out of the house and moved in with his girlfriend. At some point Dad admitted to Kevin in anger, "You have proven you can do whatever you please!" Ironically, this realization on Dad's part signaled a turn in their relationship. Kevin visited more often, and even called occasionally to ask his dad for advice. Kevin is now married, has a daughter of his own, and views his father as one of the greatest examples and supports in his life.

Watching the evolution of Kevin's relationship with his dad reminds me of a statement often attributed to Mark Twain: "When I was a boy of fourteen, my father was so ignorant I could hardly stand to have the old man around. But when I got to be twenty-one, I was astonished at how much the old man had learned in seven years." Quite often kids do come around to our way of seeing things, but they can learn only when they are ready to be taught, and sometimes pushing just defeats our purpose. Parents can't be blamed for all the bad choices of their children, but sometimes they do unintentionally nudge kids further along the path of self-destruction by trying to tighten a grip that the kids have already eluded. "Solutions" of this kind only serve to exacerbate the problem. Parents who intervene without thoughtfulness and restraint will likely raise children who are neither thoughtful nor restrained.

We stretch ourselves when we try to understand and encourage a child's unique personality. Stretching ourselves in this way leads to growth. We stretch our kids when we try to force them to fit our mold. Stretching them in this way may break the relationship. Power over our kids should never replace support for who and what they are. Power is imposed from above and requires little effort or sacrifice. Support lifts from beneath and demands observation, thoughtfulness, and selfless effort.

Take External Struggles Inside

Too often, the struggle to get kids to mind is played out on the outside—between us and them. As parents, we must do everything we can to move that conflict inside, encouraging a child to struggle with his or her own conscience. When we "take it inside" in this way, we save ourselves a lot of grief and help our kids grow in the process.

I once worked with a seventeen-year-old girl who continually fought the rules, both at home when she lived with her parents and then in the group home where she was living when I worked with her. Talking about her defiant approach to life one day, I asked her what was so difficult about following one of rules in the group home, particularly if it would bring her more privileges. "But that would mean Kimberly and Anthony (her group home parents) have won!" she protested. It hit home to me then that she viewed her relationships with authority figures as contests. If they got what they wanted, she lost; if she got what she wanted, they lost.

She had been willing to get arrested, live in a group home, and lose all her privileges there so that she wouldn't have to admit defeat in her struggle with authority figures. That's the power of the drive for independence in the teenage years. Ironically, in her fierce independence she had destroyed any opportunity for real freedom in her life.

"You're hurting yourself just to make sure Kimberly and

Anthony don't win?" I asked. "Are you really willing to sacrifice your own life just for the effect it will have on theirs?"

Over the following weeks and months, I did everything I could to turn her struggle inward. "Let's talk about what will help you win in *life,* not in some competition with your parents and group home parents," I kept reminding her. She needed to realize that her destructive actions were primarily self-destructive. Hurting the adults in her life did nothing for her in the long run (though it seemed to be quite entertaining for the time being, for some reason).

Six months later, as we wrapped up therapy and she prepared to move to an apartment of her own (she was eighteen by then), she looked back on this one thing as the most important lesson of therapy. "Now I'm putting my life first," she said, "and I've discovered that other people are actually on my side."

At home, I have tried this strategy with my younger kids and have witnessed some amazing results. It's funny, because I am often tempted to force the issue when they don't respond to my requests. For instance, I have done my share of pleading, nagging, and using bodily force to get toddlers into their car seats. But one day I decided to try an experiment. When our three-year-old didn't sit down to be strapped in, I simply sat and waited and let my request sink in. After about twenty seconds, I said, "I'm disappointed that you didn't mind by getting in your car seat." My son said, "I don't *want* to." I simply waited and let him deal with the disappointment I had expressed. I was hoping that his conscience was being pricked, that I had internalized the struggle about the car seat rather than acting it out between us. I wasn't sure this would work; after all, he was only three. But within a few seconds I saw evidence that I had triggered an internal struggle. "Dad," he said, "I don't *have* to get into my car seat!" A few more seconds went by. "I *don't!*" Then finally, in a pleading voice, *"Dad!"* Still I said nothing, ignoring his resistance. He was clearly feeling some internal tension; I didn't want to give him a chance to release it in a verbal exchange with me. Within a couple of minutes of the original request, he had had enough. "Dad, I'm in," he said as he sat down in his car seat. I couldn't believe it had worked. "Good," I responded. "Now we are all safe."

Whether they are three, seventeen, or somewhere in between, our kids shouldn't have our solutions imposed on them for conflicts that they are better off working out internally. After all, someday we won't be there to force them to do what is best. How much better off they will be then if we have let them struggle through such issues for themselves!

Stay In Charge of Yourself

Some of my best moments occur when I'm teaching parents. I present helpful material in a way that's well organized and easy to understand. Some of the ideas make sense to them and they nod in agreement. They ask me questions; I give my "expert opinion." It's a lot of fun and a great stroke to my ego. Hopefully we have a laugh or two and help each other in the process.

Times like these look nothing like my worst moments, which are usually when I'm dealing directly with kids myself. The irony of this is not lost on my ten-year-old brother-in-law, who recently shared with me this observation: "Mark, you teach people how to control their kids and you can't even control your kids."

I had one of those worst moments one cold October morning a few years ago. Ryan, then four years old, was attending the child development lab preschool at the college where I taught. Because the preschool was in the same building as my office, it was completely convenient: I would take Ryan to preschool when I went to work in the morning, and then at 10:40 I'd take an early lunch so I could drop him off at home.

It was so simple in theory. But that day, it didn't work out that way. When I got to the preschool to pick Ryan up, he ran away from me squealing and hid in a playhouse in the corner of the room. He was typically very wound up by the time he had spent three hours at preschool, so I was used to this. Usually I tried to channel his energy by wrestling with him for a minute or challenging him to a race to the car. But I didn't have much time that day, so I just stood by the door and waited. I knew that if I chased him and tried to pull him out of the playhouse, I would be in for a cat-and-mouse game that could go on for a while. My strategy worked—right away he came out, put on his coat, and got ready to go.

Something else you should know about our routine: I had learned the hard way to help Ryan release his tension by wrestling or racing. Before I started doing this on a regular basis, frequently he would explode in a tantrum somewhere between the preschool and the car. That day, his tension was evident. I hoped that I could just get him out to the car before he blew. If we could make it to the car, I knew we'd be home free. And we almost did.

However, that day it happened to be rainy and wet. We were about ten feet from the car when Ryan remembered that we had taken an umbrella with us that morning. It was a new one—the kind that opens with the push of a button—and Ryan thought it was a lot of fun.

"Daddy, we forgot the umbrella! Let's go back in and get it!"

Time for Dad to make a quick executive decision: *We're standing here in the rain, right next to the car, we'll be driving right into the garage, no chance of getting any wetter between here and home.* "No, let's go now. I'll bring it with me when I come home tonight."

That was not what Ryan wanted to hear. He stopped walking and insisted, "No, I need it. Let's just go back in and get the umbrella!"

I had the car door open by then and was climbing in to get out of the rain. "Come on, Ryan, I'll bring it home later."

"I'm not coming. I want it."

There I was, sitting in a 1973 green Dodge Dart (which attracts enough attention on its own), yelling back and forth with a four-year-old who was standing in the rain in tears.

Now, the preschool was in the same building as the psychology department *and* the family sciences department of the college, and the parking lot was directly in front of the windows to the family science offices. There was a glare on the windows, so I couldn't see in, but I could just imagine my colleagues—the family science professors—gathering to look out.

"Look."

"What's that? No, you're right, he's a psychologist."

"No, you're right, he specializes in child psychology."

"No, you're right, his son is only four."

"No, you're right, he's writing a book on raising kids."

With these imaginary comments in mind, I decided to end this scene—or at least take it home where I could be inept in privacy. So I got out of my car and walked over to where Ryan was standing. As I approached, he ran away. I started to chase him but stopped myself, realizing that a footrace on the slippery pavement might just take this vaudeville act to an entirely new level. So I walked back and got in the car. And hoped and prayed that Ryan would come back. I even started to back the car out, hoping in my anger that the threat of abandonment would coerce him into cooperation.

He did return. But not all the way. He stood about four feet from the door on the passenger's side of the car.

Ruth, the secretary of the psychology department, had a granddaughter in the same preschool as Ryan. As luck would have it, at that moment, Ruth, her daughter, and her granddaughter were exiting the building. Just that week I had shared with Ruth an article I had written on "Staying In Charge When Kids Push the Limits." She had given a photocopy to her daughter, who had apparently already read the article and gained a lot from it. After all, her little girl was being a perfect angel. Seeing my dilemma, Ruth stopped and made an attempt to coax Ryan into the car. He didn't budge.

I reached over and opened the door on the passenger's side. Ryan maintained his distance, crying and pleading about the umbrella. "Dad, if I ask 'please' can we get it?" In the midst of this emotional storm, he was doing his best to handle the problem in the way we had tried to teach him to. I wondered, *If it's that important to him, is all this really worth it?* But I had dug a nice little hole for myself: If I went in to get the umbrella at this point, wouldn't we be in for a bigger tantrum the next time he didn't get his way? He really would be in charge of family life then.

My heart went out to him, but I was also still very upset myself. "No. Get in the car!"

As he stood there pleading and stomping and crying, he gradually inched my way. When he was within reach, I lunged over, grabbed him by his jacket, and pulled him into the car.

Although I can look back now and laugh, at the time I was furious; I felt like hitting him. I am embarrassed to even write that, but at that moment it was true. Fortunately, I restrained myself. I told him a couple of times on the way home how angry I was that he hadn't minded. I took my anger out on the front door when we got home—slammed it as I walked into the house—and ordered Ryan to his room with the threat of a spanking if he didn't go.

I told Jenny the story in a nutshell, asked her not to let him out for an hour, and slammed the door again on my way out of the house. I went back to the office without lunch—I was too upset to eat. I felt terrible inside, a mixture of frustration, guilt, and compassion for Ryan's struggle with his emotions.

Fifteen minutes later, having calmed down, I called Jenny and asked her to shorten Ryan's punishment to half an hour. We talked for a while and I told her more of the story. We shared a couple of ideas about handling problems like this in the future. Talking it out helped to soothe my nerves. Twenty minutes later I called again and talked with Ryan. We made up over the phone. That night when I got home, I spent some time with him. It seemed that we were back in each other's good graces.

I find that even thinking back on the events of that day makes me feel uncomfortable again. It was the most frustrated I have ever been as a parent. As I write it out, I find myself wanting to write about how I handled such a problem better the next time. After all, most of my stories about strategies that work were preceded by countless experiences with failure and frustration—though most have been on a smaller scale than what occurred that day. For that matter, why include the story in the book at all? Maybe it would be better if I just put it behind me and tried to forget the whole thing.

But I can't do that. That experience was significant for me because it occurred even after ten years of training, education, and experience working with kids and their problem behavior. It reminds me that learning can't solve all the problems we face with our kids, that no matter how much we think we know, at times we still reach the end of our rope.

The experience also reminded me that we can't always stay in charge of our children. Sometimes the best strategies and the best intentions break down. That's not necessarily all bad. Kids are individual people, and ultimately they exercise their power. At times it's frustrating, but they do have minds and lives of their own.

Ultimately, there is one thing about that experience of which I am proud: I restrained my urge to hit my child. What we do in situations when we're not in charge is just as important as what we do when we are. When we lose control of our kids, that's when it's most important to stay in control of ourselves.

Of course, I wasn't completely in control that day. Some would say I was "emotionally abusive." I hope Ryan wasn't traumatized by *my* temper tantrum. I was doing the best I could at the time, but that incident made me think long and hard. It motivated me to find ways to calm myself when I feel myself starting to get angry. Now I breathe deeply and remind myself that no single incident is the end of the world.

Some of the strategies in this book will help prevent and solve problems like the one I faced that day. But no matter how hard we try, some problems are inevitable. Sometimes nothing works. At such times, avoiding child abuse might be the best we can do.

In the heat of the moment, we may feel that we *must* win the battle with our kids, no matter the cost. Irrationally, we think we have to make a strong statement this time or all is lost. But usually, that's just not true. Remember, child rearing is a marathon with hurdles, not a sprint. If we know where we want to go and keep at it, eventually our kids will learn to comply with our rules and directions. They'll be much better off if they can get there without having suffered the trauma of abuse.

Not All Conflicts Are Power Struggles

For years, I kept having power struggles with my oldest son. I was determined to get him to mind; he was determined not to, or at least so it seemed. Then one day I realized that this was all about power to me only. To him, it was at least partly about knowledge.

Let me explain. One evening after we had returned home late from a trip, I asked seven-year-old Ryan to feed his guinea pig before he went to bed. I came into the family room ten minutes later to find him holding his pet on the couch. I told him to put "Guinea" away and go to bed.

"No, Dad, I—"

I cut his explanation short. "Ryan, this is the last time I'll ask you; then you'll lose a privilege."

"Dad!" he protested with a distressed look on his face, his frustration and anger clearly building.

At that moment, Jenny walked in the room. "What's the matter?" she asked. *What does she mean, what's the matter?* I thought. *Can't she see he is pushing the limits, testing my authority? What's the matter with the way I'm handling this?*

At her invitation, Ryan said, "I was trying to tell Dad about how it makes a guinea pig be your friend if you feed it by hand." (*Bond* and *imprint* were the words the library book used, Jenny explained later—and yes, it was true.)

Jenny said simply, "Ryan, Guinea is real lucky to have an owner who understands him like you do, but tonight Mom and Dad are tired, and we can't go to bed until you do. Do you think he would be okay if tonight you just put the food in his cage, and then fed him by hand first thing in the morning?"

Ryan nodded and complied with her request. "I don't think he will mind. Plus, if we turn the light off he will know it is night," he suggested.

As I watched Jenny work that magic, it occurred to me: Ryan was more focused on his understanding of guinea pigs than on my authority. He responded best to a parent who was on the same page with him. Jenny knew what his need was and tried to meet it. Once his understanding was acknowledged and he was allowed to give it voice, he went to bed without putting up a fight.

So that was it! Ryan didn't really care about staying up against my orders, at least not that night. He just didn't want what he knew to be ignored or dismissed.

Ryan has always tried to learn the truth about things. Once he does, he remembers factual tidbits forever, the kind of things I forget the moment I learn them. And he enjoys teaching others about what he has learned. This is the way he shines in our family. He is "the scientist," just as one of his brothers is "the helper" and another is "the clown." I knew Ryan was going to be a scientist the day he looked at the tree in our neighbor's yard and asked, "Dad, does that tree have compound leaves or simple leaves?" Huh? I couldn't bluff on that one. "Ryan," I said, "you'll have to teach me about how to tell the difference, and then we can figure it out together." (Turns out the plum tree had simple leaves.)

Because of his interest in learning, I should have discerned even sooner that it might be the cause of some of our conflicts. But I was so focused on the issue of power, I was blind to it. I don't even want to think about how many of our previous "power struggles" had resulted from my refusal to acknowledge Ryan's understanding because I thought he was simply defying my authority. How often had he just been trying to show me that he knew something neat? Judging by how often I have seen this issue come up since my perspective shifted, I'm afraid I missed the boat many a time.

When Ryan lags behind the rest of us at Dinosaur Park, he's not trying to exert control by slowing us down. He has no interest in making the rest of us wait. We're the last thing on his mind. He's busy explaining to some of the other patrons the virtues of his favorite prehistoric beast, the Ankylosaurus. "Dad, they didn't know that little guy could sometimes even beat the T-Rex," he informed me when he caught up with us again. "I showed 'em the club on his tail and how his body armor is like an army tank."

Likewise, when he clicked the car doors unlocked after I thought I had them locked, he wasn't just being a tease. And he wasn't trying to pick a fight, as I might have assumed before. He was showing me that he was smart enough to do something I thought only the adults in our family could do. When I said, "Hey, I didn't know you knew how to do that!" Ryan flashed me a smile and locked them up again.

We have fewer fights now that I know he often just wants to be heard, wants to have his intelligence acknowledged. This has been an amazing demonstration to me that some "power struggles" simply evaporate when we recognize that they might be over something other than power.

Life Is Not All About Who's In Charge

ecently I was involved in a discussion with other parents about
children and boundaries. Parents in all stages of child rearing
commiserated about how hard it is to set limits and stick to them.

What do you do when a child rebels? How much say should
children have in making the rules? When are children old enough
to make decisions for themselves? My favorite question was from a
tired-looking father of two, a toddler and an infant: "Once you've
drawn a line, can you ever change your mind? If not, is consistency worth the price of sanity?"

Regardless of our various parenting styles, it seems we all
struggle with the issue of setting limits. It was nice to see parents
supporting and learning from each other. As the discussion went
on, however, I started to feel uneasy. Due as much to the tone of
the discussion as the topic, I began to feel like we were military
officers, locked away in command headquarters, plotting the final
overthrow of a vicious enemy. That was when it hit me: Setting
limits is only about 10 percent of what we do as parents, if that.
And we would be a lot less stressed out if we focused on the other
90 percent a little more.

Before I talk about that 90 percent of parenting beyond limit
setting, I'll concede several points about the importance of restrictions:

Children seem compelled to test boundaries and "push the
limits."

Firmness goes hand in hand with love—they are not opposite ends of one continuum.

Boundaries and guidelines provide children with a sense that the world is a predictable, safe place.

Having admitted those points, I now feel free to say that setting boundaries is not nearly as important as many other things we do with our children. Imagine a football game as a metaphor for our lives with our kids. What if you turned on the TV one Saturday morning to find that the commentators spent all their time talking about the rules of the game? What if they focused more on the out-of-bounds lines than on what was happening on the field? Rules add to the game by maintaining order, preventing chaos. However, the real intrigue of the game is in what the players are allowed to do, not what they're kept from doing. When violations occur, the referee steps in, delivers the consequence, and gets on with the game as quickly as possible. He doesn't spend time haggling over the details of the violation. And he doesn't play the martyr: "How many times have I told you not to foul? Haven't I taught you well enough? Am I not a good referee? You don't appreciate me!"

This point about spending more time enjoying the game hit home for me once when I was taking a walk with Ryan, who was two years old at the time. We were walking on a beautiful bike path along an area that had just been landscaped. Ryan and I were both enjoying the landscaping; I admired it visually, while Ryan preferred to gain a more tactile appreciation. I turned to see that he had squatted down by a seedling and was stripping the leaves off its tender branches. I ran over and stopped him, of course, but he was not easily diverted. At first I held his wrists and kept his hands from the victimized plant. When that didn't work, I stood between him and the tiny tree, dodging back and forth to block his charges. In the midst of this boundary struggle, I looked across to the other side of the path and realized there was an entire field of weeds over there that no one cared about. Within seconds the struggle was over as I led him to the field and gave him free reign. We had a ball together, tromping through the grass and pulling up weeds to his heart's content.

As I think about that incident, I realize that the most memorable experiences from my own childhood have nothing to do with limits and boundaries. Sure, there was conflict between me and my parents. I remember some real struggles over whether I would continue school beyond the fourth grade, how late I could stay out, and how much of my dress and grooming was their business. But what stand out the most are times like working on a wood project or going to get a milkshake with Dad, taking family trips together in the summer, or going to the grocery store with Mom. We would always stop by the bakery, and she'd let me choose a cookie. I liked the pastel-colored ones with sprinkles on top, the ones that are mostly lard and sugar. Funny, I don't remember screaming at the checkout stand, although I'm sure I probably did that, too. But I can still taste those pastel cookies with sprinkles.

When we are dealing with problems—when our kids are whining, quarreling, throwing tantrums, or resisting—let us remember that this is not all of life, or even the most important part. Grandma's house, yard work, airplanes taking off, trips to the museum, camping adventures, walks as a family—these are the things that will stand out in their memories of childhood. So let's not allow the challenges and problems to absorb all of our mental energy, either. We can appreciate who our kids are now even as we try to help them become better people. We can enjoy a wonderful family life in the midst of dealing with the typical troubles. We will discover that even referees can enjoy the game if, in addition to enforcing the rules, we let our kids play ball.

Index